THE LAW OF PEOPLES

THE LAW OF PEOPLES

with "The Idea of Public Reason Revisited"

JOHN RAWLS

HARVARD UNIVERSITY PRESS
Cambridge, Massachusetts
London, England 1999

Library of Congress Cataloging-in-Publication Data

Rawls, John, 1921–
  [Law of peoples]
  The law of peoples ; with, The idea of public reason revisited / John Rawls.
    p.   cm.
  Includes bibliographical references and index.
  ISBN 0-674-00079-X (alk. paper)
  1. International relations—Philosophy.   2. Social justice.   3. Social contract.
  4. Liberalism.   5. Toleration.   I. Rawls, John, 1921–   Idea of public reason revisited.
  II. Title.   III. Title: Law of peoples ; with , The idea of public reason revisited.
  IV. Title: Idea of public reason revisited.
JZ1242.R39   1999
320.51—dc21
                                                                            99-34785

Preface

Since the late 1980s I have thought occasionally of developing what I have called "The Law of Peoples." I first chose the name "peoples" rather than "nations" or "states" because I wanted to conceive of peoples as having different features from those of states, since the idea of states, as traditionally conceived with their two powers of sovereignty (see §2.2), was unsuitable. In the next years I devoted more time to the topic, and on February 12, 1993 —Lincoln's birthday—I delivered an Oxford Amnesty Lecture entitled "The Law of Peoples." The lecture provided an occasion on which to remind the audience of Lincoln's greatness (which I did in my conclusion), but I was never satisfied with what I said or did with the published essay (the original version was published in the volume *On Human Rights: The Oxford Amnesty Lectures, 1993,* ed. Stephen Shute and Susan Hurley [New York: Basic Books, 1993]). It wasn't feasible to try to cover so much in a single lecture, and what I did cover was not fully developed and was open to misinterpretation. The present version, completed during 1997–1998 (a rewriting of three seminars I gave at Princeton University in April 1995), is fuller and more satisfactory.

Prior to the final reworking of the manuscript, I completed "The Idea of Public Reason Revisited," which originally appeared in the *University of Chicago Law Review,* 64 (Summer 1997), and subsequently was included in my *Collected Papers* published by Harvard

University Press (1999). That essay is my most detailed account of why the constraints of public reason, as manifested in a modern constitutional democracy based on a liberal political conception (an idea first discussed in *Political Liberalism* in 1993), are ones that holders of both religious and nonreligious comprehensive views can reasonably endorse. The idea of public reason is also integral to the Law of Peoples, which extends the idea of a social contract to the Society of Peoples, and lays out the general principles that can and should be accepted by both liberal and nonliberal (but decent) societies as the standard for regulating their behavior toward one another. For this reason, I wanted to have the two works published in the same volume. Taken together, they represent the culmination of my reflections on how reasonable citizens and peoples might live together peacefully in a just world.

Those who have helped me over the years in bringing these thoughts to fruition are too numerous to mention, though I do want to thank especially Erin Kelly, T. M. Scanlon, Percy Lehning, Thomas Pogge, and Charles Beitz. I want them all to know how much I appreciate the time they spent reviewing the many drafts of this work, and how much I have depended on their thoughtful comments.

I must also give special thanks to Samuel Freeman, who, after editing my *Collected Papers* and producing its index, agreed to index this work—another enormous task. He has done a remarkable job, thorough and professional.

Finally, I owe an extraordinary debt of thanks to my dear friend and colleague Burton Dreben, who died this past July. Burt has always been enormously helpful to me as I developed my ideas, organizing and clearing up my thoughts, and cutting off those that seemed to lead to confusion. During the last three years since my illness he, together with my wife, Mardy, has been tireless in pushing me to finish the works, and in offering countless, careful editorial suggestions as successive drafts were produced. To Burt I am, as always, endlessly grateful.

Contents

THE IDEA OF PUBLIC REASON REVISITED   129

THE
LAW OF
PEOPLES

Introduction

1. By the "Law of Peoples"[1] I mean a particular political conception of right and justice that applies to the principles and norms of international law and practice. I shall use the term "Society of Peoples" to mean all those peoples who follow the ideals and principles of the Law of Peoples in their mutual relations. These peoples have their own internal governments, which may be constitutional liberal democratic or nonliberal but decent[2] governments. In this book I consider how the content of the Law of Peoples might be developed out of a liberal idea of justice similar to, but more general than, the idea I called *justice as fairness*[3]

1. The term "law of peoples" derives from the traditional *ius gentium,* and the phrase *ius gentium intra se* refers to what the laws of all peoples have in common. See R. J. Vincent, *Human Rights and International Relations* (Cambridge and New York: Cambridge University Press, 1986), p. 27. I do not use the term "law of peoples" with this meaning, however, but rather to mean the particular political principles for regulating the mutual political relations between peoples, as defined in §2.

2. I use the term "decent" to describe nonliberal societies whose basic institutions meet certain specified conditions of political right and justice (including the right of citizens to play a substantial role, say through associations and groups, in making political decisions) and lead their citizens to honor a reasonably just law for the Society of Peoples. The idea is discussed at length in Part II. My use of the term differs from that of Avishai Margalit, who emphasizes consideration of social welfare in *The Decent Society* (Cambridge, Mass.: Harvard University Press, 1996).

3. By the italics I mean to signify that "justice as fairness" is the name of a particular conception of justice. Subsequently italics will not be used.

in *A Theory of Justice* (1971). This idea of justice is based on the familiar idea of the social contract, and the procedure followed before the principles of right and justice are selected and agreed upon is in some ways the same in both the domestic and the international case. I shall discuss how such a Law of Peoples[4] fulfills certain conditions, which justify calling the Society of Peoples a *realistic utopia* (see §1), and I shall also return to and explain why I have used the term "peoples" and not "states."[5]

In §58 of *A Theory of Justice* I indicated how justice as fairness can be extended to international law (as I called it there) for the limited purpose of judging the aims and limits of just war. Here my discussion covers more ground. I propose considering five types of domestic societies. The first is *reasonable liberal peoples;* the second, *decent peoples* (see note 2 above). The basic structure of one kind of decent people has what I call a "decent consultation hierarchy," and these peoples I call "decent hierarchical peoples." Other possible kinds of decent peoples I do not try to describe, but simply leave in reserve, allowing that there may be other decent peoples whose basic structure does not fit my description of a consultation hierarchy, but who are worthy of membership in a Society of Peoples. (Liberal peoples and decent peoples I refer to together as "well-ordered peoples.")[6] There are, third, *outlaw states* and, fourth, *societies burdened by unfavorable conditions.* Finally, fifth, we have societies that are *benevolent absolutisms:* they honor human rights; but, because their members are denied a meaningful role in making political decisions, they are not well-ordered.

The account of the extension of a general social contract idea to a Society of Peoples will unfold in three parts, covering both what I have called ideal and nonideal theory. The first part of ideal theory in Part I concerns the extension of the general social contract idea to the

4. Throughout this book I will sometimes refer to *a* Law of Peoples, and sometimes to *the* Law of Peoples. As will become clear, there is no single possible Law of Peoples, but rather a family of reasonable such laws meeting all the conditions and criteria I will discuss, and satisfying the representatives of peoples who will be determining the specifics of the law.

5. In §2 I explain the meaning of "peoples" more fully.

6. The term "well-ordered" comes from Jean Bodin, who at the beginning of his *Six Books of the Republic* (1576) refers to the "*République bien ordonnée.*"

society of liberal democratic peoples. The second part of ideal theory in Part II concerns the extension of the same idea to the society of decent peoples, which, though they are not liberal democratic societies, have certain features making them acceptable as members in good standing in a reasonable Society of Peoples. The ideal theory part of the extension of the social contract idea is completed by showing that both kinds of societies, liberal and decent, would agree to the same Law of Peoples. A Society of Peoples is reasonably just in that its members follow the reasonably just Law of Peoples in their mutual relations.

An aim of Part II is to show that there may exist decent nonliberal peoples who accept and follow the Law of Peoples. To this end I give an imagined example of a nonliberal Muslim people I call "Kazanistan." This people satisfies the criteria for decent hierarchical peoples I set forth (§§8–9): Kazanistan is not aggressive against other peoples and accepts and follows the Law of Peoples; it honors and respects human rights; and its basic structure contains a decent consultation hierarchy, the features of which I describe.

Part III takes up the two kinds of nonideal theory. One kind deals with conditions of noncompliance, that is, with conditions in which certain regimes refuse to comply with a reasonable Law of Peoples. These we may call outlaw states, and I discuss what measures other societies—liberal peoples or decent peoples—may justifiably take to defend themselves against them. The other kind of nonideal theory deals with unfavorable conditions, that is, with the conditions of societies whose historical, social, and economic circumstances make their achieving a well-ordered regime, whether liberal or decent, difficult if not impossible. In regard to these burdened societies we must ask how far liberal or decent peoples owe a duty of assistance to these societies so that the latter may establish their own reasonably just or decent institutions. The aim of the Law of Peoples would be fully achieved when all societies have been able to establish either a liberal or a decent regime, however unlikely that may be.

2. This monograph on the Law of Peoples is neither a treatise nor a textbook on international law. Rather, it is a work that focuses strictly on certain questions connected with whether a realistic utopia is pos-

sible, and the conditions under which it might obtain. I begin and end with the idea of a realistic utopia. Political philosophy is realistically utopian when it extends what are ordinarily thought of as the limits of practical political possibility. Our hope for the future of our society rests on the belief that the nature of the social world allows reasonably just constitutional democratic societies existing as members of the Society of Peoples. In such a social world peace and justice would be achieved between liberal and decent peoples both at home and abroad. The idea of this society is realistically utopian in that it depicts an achievable social world that combines political right and justice for all liberal and decent peoples in a Society of Peoples. Both *A Theory of Justice* and *Political Liberalism* try to say how a liberal society might be possible.[7] *The Law of Peoples* hopes to say how a world Society of liberal and decent Peoples might be possible. Of course, many would say that it is not possible, and that utopian elements may be a serious defect in a society's political culture.[8]

On the contrary, though I would not deny that such elements can be misconceived, I believe the idea of a realistic utopia is essential. Two main ideas motivate the Law of Peoples. One is that the great evils of

7. See *Political Liberalism* (New York: Columbia University Press, 1993) and the paperback edition of 1996 with a second introduction and the "Reply to Habermas," first published in the *Journal of Philosophy,* March 1995. My present remarks draw on the closing paragraphs of the second introduction.

8. I am thinking here of E. H. Carr's *The Twenty Year Crisis, 1919–1939: An Introduction to the Study of International Relations* (London: Macmillan, 1951) and his well-known criticism of utopian thought. (My citations are from the Harper Torchbook edition of 1964.) Carr may have been right that utopian thinking, in his sense, played an adverse role in the policies of England and France in the interwar period and contributed to bringing about World War II. See his chapters 4 and 5, which criticize the idea of a "harmony of interests." Carr's idea of the harmony of interests, however, refers not to philosophy, but rather to the wishful thinking of powerful politicians. So, for example, Winston Churchill once remarked that "the fortunes of the British Empire and its glory are inseparably interwoven with the fortunes of the world" (p. 82). Though criticizing utopianism, Carr never questioned the essential role of moral judgment in forming our political opinions; he presented reasonable political opinions as a *compromise* between both realism (power) and utopianism (moral judgment and values). In contradistinction to Carr, my idea of a realistic utopia doesn't settle for a compromise between power and political right and justice, but sets limits to the reasonable exercise of power. Otherwise, power itself determines what the compromise should be, as Carr recognized (p. 222).

human history—unjust war and oppression, religious persecution and the denial of liberty of conscience, starvation and poverty, not to mention genocide and mass murder—follow from political injustice, with its own cruelties and callousness. (Here the idea of political justice is the same as that discussed by political liberalism,[9] out of which the Law of Peoples is developed.) The other main idea, obviously connected with the first, is that, once the gravest forms of political injustice are eliminated by following just (or at least decent) social policies and establishing just (or at least decent) basic institutions, these great evils will eventually disappear. I connect these ideas to the idea of a realistic utopia. Following Rousseau's opening thought in *The Social Contract* (quoted below in Part I, §1.2), I shall assume that his phrase "men as they are" refers to persons' moral and psychological natures and how that nature works within a framework of political and social institutions;[10] and that his phrase "laws as they might be" refers to laws as they should, or ought, to be. I shall also assume that, if we grow up under a framework of reasonable and just political and social institutions, we shall affirm those institutions when we in our turn come of age, and they will endure over time. In this context, to say that human nature is good is to say that citizens who grow up under reasonable and just institutions—institutions that satisfy any of a family of reasonable liberal political conceptions of justice—will affirm those institutions and act to make sure their social world endures. (As a distinguishing feature, all members of this family of conceptions satisfy the criterion of *reciprocity*.)[11] There may not be many such institutions, but, if there are, they must be ones that we can understand and act on, approve, and endorse. I contend that this scenario is realistic—it could and may exist. I say it is also utopian and highly desirable because it joins reasonableness and justice with conditions enabling citizens to realize their fundamental interests.

9. See "The Idea of Public Reason Revisited" in the present volume, especially pp. 131–148.

10. Rousseau also said: "The limits of the possible in moral matters are less narrow than we think. It is our weaknesses, our vices, our prejudices, that shrink them. Base souls do not believe in great men. Vile slaves smile mockingly at the word freedom." See *The Social Contract*, book II, chap. 12, para. 2.

11. See "The Idea of Public Reason Revisited," pp. 132, 136–138.

3. As a consequence of focusing on the idea of a realistic utopia, many of the immediate problems of contemporary foreign policy that trouble citizens and politicians will be left aside altogether or treated only briefly. I note three important examples: unjust war, immigration, and nuclear and other weapons of mass destruction.

The crucial fact for the problem of war is that constitutional democratic societies do not go to war with one another (§5). This is not because the citizenry of such societies is peculiarly just and good, but more simply because they have no cause to go to war with one another. Compare democratic societies with the nation-states of the earlier modern period in Europe. England, France, Spain, Hapsburg Austria, Sweden, and others fought dynastic wars for territory, true religion, for power and glory, and a place in the sun. These were wars of Monarchs and Royal Houses; the internal institutional structure of these societies made them inherently aggressive and hostile to other states. The crucial fact of peace among democracies rests on the *internal* structure of democratic societies, which are not tempted to go to war except in self-defense or in grave cases of intervention in unjust societies to protect human rights. Since constitutional democratic societies are safe from each other, peace reigns among them.

Concerning the second problem, immigration, in §4.3 I argue that an important role of government, however arbitrary a society's boundaries may appear from a historical point of view, is to be the effective agent of a people as they take responsibility for their territory and the size of their population, as well as for maintaining the land's environmental integrity. Unless a definite agent is given responsibility for maintaining an asset and bears the responsibility and loss for not doing so, that asset tends to deteriorate. On my account the role of the institution of property is to prevent this deterioration from occurring. In the present case, the asset is the people's territory and its potential capacity to support them *in perpetuity;* and the agent is the people itself as politically organized. The perpetuity condition is crucial. People must recognize that they cannot make up for failing to regulate their numbers or to care for their land by conquest in war, or by migrating into another people's territory without their consent.

There are numerous causes of immigration. I mention several and suggest that they would disappear in the Society of liberal and decent Peoples. One is the persecution of religious and ethnic minorities, the denial of their human rights. Another is political oppression of various forms, as when the members of the peasant classes are conscripted and hired out by monarchs as mercenaries in their dynastic wars for power and territory.[12] Often people are simply fleeing from starvation, as in the Irish famine of the 1840s. Yet famines are often themselves in large part caused by political failures and the absence of decent government.[13] The last cause I mention is population pressure in the home territory, and among its complex of causes is the inequality and subjection of women. Once that inequality and subjection are overcome, and women are granted equal political participation with men and assured education, these problems can be resolved. Thus, religious freedom and liberty of conscience, political freedom and constitutional liberties, and equal justice for women are fundamental aspects of sound social policy for a realistic utopia (see §15.3–4). The problem of immigration is not, then, simply left aside, but is eliminated as a serious problem in a realistic utopia.

I shall only briefly mention the question of controlling nuclear weapons and other weapons of mass destruction. Among reasonably just liberal and decent peoples the control of such weapons would be relatively easy, since they could be effectively banned. These peoples have no reason for going to war with one another. Yet so long as there are outlaw states—as we suppose—some nuclear weapons need to be retained to keep those states at bay and to make sure they do not obtain and use those weapons against liberal or decent peoples. How best to do this belongs to expert knowledge, which philosophy doesn't possess. There remains, of course, the great moral question of whether, and in what circumstances, nuclear weapons can be used at all (see the discussion in §14).

4. Finally, it is important to see that the Law of Peoples is developed within political liberalism and is an extension of a liberal conception of justice for a domestic regime to a Society of Peoples. I emphasize

12. Think of the Hessian troops who deserted the British Army and became citizens of the United States after the American Revolution.

13. See note 35 on Amartya Sen, Part III, §15.3.

that, in developing the Law of Peoples within a liberal conception of justice, we work out the ideals and principles of the *foreign policy* of a reasonably just *liberal* people. This concern with the foreign policy of a liberal people is implicit throughout. The reason we go on to consider the point of view of decent peoples is not to prescribe principles of justice for *them,* but to assure ourselves that the ideals and principles of the foreign policy of a liberal people are also reasonable from a decent nonliberal point of view. The need for such assurance is a feature inherent in the liberal conception. The Law of Peoples holds that decent nonliberal points of view exist, and that the question of how far nonliberal peoples are to be tolerated is an essential question of liberal foreign policy.

The basic idea is to follow Kant's lead as sketched by him in *Perpetual Peace* (1795) and his idea of *foedus pacificum.* I interpret this idea to mean that we are to begin with the social contract idea of the liberal political conception of a constitutionally democratic regime and then extend it by introducing a second original position at the second level, so to speak, in which the representatives of liberal peoples make an agreement with other liberal peoples. This I do in §§3–4, and again later with nonliberal though decent peoples in §§8–9. Each of these agreements is understood as hypothetical and nonhistorical, and entered into by equal peoples symmetrically situated in the original position behind an appropriate veil of ignorance. Hence the undertaking between peoples is fair. All this also accords with Kant's idea that a constitutional regime must establish an effective Law of Peoples in order to realize fully the freedom of its citizens.[14] I cannot be sure in advance that this approach to the Law of Peoples will work out, nor do I maintain that other ways of arriving at the Law of Peoples are incorrect. Should there be other ways to arrive at the same place, so much the better.

14. See *Theory and Practice,* part III: Ak:VIII:308–310, where Kant considers theory in relation to the practice of international right, or as he says, from a cosmopolitan point of view; and *Idea for a Universal History,* Seventh Proposition, Ak:VIII:24ff.

The First Part of Ideal Theory

§1. The Law of Peoples as Realistic Utopia

1.1. Meaning of Realistic Utopia. As I stated in the Introduction, political philosophy is realistically utopian when it extends what are ordinarily thought to be the limits of practicable political possibility and, in so doing, reconciles us to our political and social condition. Our hope for the future of our society rests on the belief that the social world allows a reasonably just constitutional democracy existing as a member of a reasonably just Society of Peoples. What would a reasonably just constitutional democracy be like under reasonably favorable historical conditions that are possible given the laws and tendencies of society? And how do these conditions relate to laws and tendencies bearing on the relations between peoples?

These historical conditions include, in a reasonably just domestic society, the fact of reasonable pluralism.[1] In the Society of Peoples, the parallel to reasonable pluralism is the diversity among reasonable peoples with their different cultures and traditions of thought, both religious and nonreligious. Even when two or more peoples have liberal constitutional regimes, their conceptions of constitutionalism may diverge and express different variations of liberalism. A (reasonable) Law

1. See the definition on p. 36 of *Political Liberalism*. See also "The Idea of Public Reason Revisited" in the present volume.

of Peoples must be acceptable to reasonable peoples who are thus diverse; and it must be fair between them and effective in shaping the larger schemes of their cooperation.

This fact of reasonable pluralism limits what is practicably possible here and now, whatever may have been the case in other historical ages when, it is often said, people within a domestic society were united (though perhaps they never really have been) in affirming one comprehensive doctrine. I recognize that there are questions about how the limits of the practicably possible are discerned and what the conditions of our social world in fact are. The problem here is that the limits of the possible are not given by the actual, for we can to a greater or lesser extent change political and social institutions and much else. Hence we have to rely on conjecture and speculation, arguing as best we can that the social world we envision is feasible and might actually exist, if not now then at some future time under happier circumstances.

Eventually we want to ask whether reasonable pluralism within or between peoples is a historical condition to which we should be reconciled. Though we can imagine what we sometimes think would be a happier world—one in which everyone, or all peoples, have the same faith that we do—that is not the question, excluded as it is by the nature and culture of free institutions. To show that reasonable pluralism is not to be regretted, we must show that, given the socially feasible alternatives, the existence of reasonable pluralism allows a society of greater political justice and liberty. To argue this cogently would be to reconcile us to our contemporary political and social condition.

1.2. Conditions of the Domestic Case. I begin with a sketch of a reasonably just constitutional democratic society (hereafter sometimes referred to simply as a liberal society) as a realistic utopia and review seven conditions that are necessary for such a realistic utopia to obtain. Then I check whether parallel conditions would hold for a society of reasonably just and decent peoples who honor a Law of Peoples. Should those conditions also hold, the Society of Peoples is also a case of realistic utopia.

(i) There are two necessary conditions for a liberal conception of justice to be *realistic.* The first is that it must rely on the actual laws of nature and achieve the kind of stability those laws allow, that is, stability for the right reasons.[2] It takes people as they are (by the laws of nature), and constitutional and civil laws as they might be, that is, as they would be in a reasonably just and well-ordered democratic society. Here I follow Rousseau's opening thought in *The Social Contract:*

> My purpose is to consider if, in political society, there can be any legitimate and sure principle of government, taking men as they are and laws as they might be. In this inquiry I shall try always to bring together what right permits with what interest requires so that justice and utility are in no way divided.

The second condition for a liberal political conception of justice to be realistic is that its first principles and precepts be workable and applicable to ongoing political and social arrangements. Here an example may be helpful: consider primary goods (basic rights and liberties, opportunities, income and wealth, and the social bases of self-respect) as used in justice as fairness. One of their main features is that they are workable. A citizen's share of these goods is openly observable and makes possible the required comparisons between citizens (so-called interpersonal comparisons). This can be done without appealing to such unworkable ideas as a people's overall utility, or to Sen's basic capabilities for various functionings (as he calls them).[3]

2. Stability for the right reasons means stability brought about by citizens acting correctly according to the appropriate principles of their sense of justice, which they have acquired by growing up under and participating in just institutions.

3. It doesn't follow, however, that Sen's idea of basic capabilities is not important here; and indeed, the contrary is the case. His thought is that society must look to the distribution of citizens' effective basic freedoms, as these are more fundamental for their lives than what they possess in primary goods, since citizens have different capabilities and skills in using those goods to achieve desirable ways of living their lives. The reply from the side of primary goods is to grant this claim—indeed, any use of primary goods must make certain simplifying assumptions about citizens' capabilities—but also to answer that to apply the idea of effective basic capabilities without those or similar assumptions calls for more information than political society can conceivably acquire and sensibly apply. Instead, by embedding primary goods into the specification of the principles of justice and ordering the basic structure of society accordingly, we may come as close as we can in practice to a just distribution of Sen's effective freedoms. His idea is essential because it is needed to explain the propriety of the use of primary goods. For Amartya Sen's view see his *Inequality Reexamined* (Cambridge, Mass.: Harvard University Press, 1992), esp. chapters 1–5.

(ii) A necessary condition for a political conception of justice to be *utopian* is that it use political (moral) ideals, principles, and concepts to specify a reasonable and just society. There is a family of reasonable liberal conceptions of justice, each of which has the following three characteristic principles:

the first enumerates basic rights and liberties of the kind familiar from a constitutional regime;

the second assigns these rights, liberties, and opportunities a special priority, especially with respect to the claims of the general good and perfectionism values; and

the third assures for all citizens the requisite primary goods to enable them to make intelligent and effective use of their freedoms.

The principles of these conceptions of justice must also satisfy the criterion of reciprocity. This criterion requires that, when terms are proposed as the most reasonable terms of fair cooperation, those proposing them must think it at least reasonable for others to accept them, as free and equal citizens, and not as dominated or manipulated or under pressure caused by an inferior political or social position.[4] Citizens will differ as to which of these conceptions they think the most reasonable, but they should be able to agree that all are reasonable, even if barely so. Each of these liberalisms endorses the underlying ideas of citizens as free and equal persons and of society as a fair system of cooperation over time. Yet since these ideas can be interpreted in various ways, we get different formulations of the principles of justice and different contents of public reason.[5] Political conceptions differ also in how they order, or balance, political principles and values even when they specify the same principles and values as significant. These liberalisms contain substantive principles of justice, and hence cover more than procedural justice. The principles are re-

4. See *Political Liberalism,* II: §1, pp. 48–54, and "The Idea of Public Reason Revisited," pp. 136ff.

5. Of these liberalisms, justice as fairness is the most egalitarian. See *Political Liberalism,* pp. 6ff.

quired to specify the religious liberties and freedoms of artistic expression of free and equal citizens, as well as substantive ideas of fairness assuring fair opportunity and adequate all-purpose means, and much else.[6]

(iii) A third condition for a realistic utopia requires that the category of the political must contain within itself all the essential elements for a political conception of justice. For example, in political liberalism persons are viewed as citizens, and a political conception of justice is built up from political (moral) ideas available in the public political culture of a liberal constitutional regime. The idea of a free citizen is determined by a liberal political conception and not by any comprehensive doctrine, which always extends beyond the category of the political.

(iv) Because of the fact of reasonable pluralism, constitutional democracy must have political and social institutions that effectively lead its citizens to acquire the appropriate sense of justice as they grow up and take part in society. They will then be able to understand the principles and ideals of the political conception, to interpret and apply them to cases at hand, and they will normally be moved to act from them as circumstances require. This leads to stability for the right reasons.

Insofar as liberal conceptions require virtuous conduct of citizens, the necessary (political) virtues are those of political cooperation, such as a sense of fairness and tolerance and a willingness to meet others halfway. Moreover, liberal political principles and ideals can be satisfied by the basic structure of society even if numerous citizens lapse on occasion, provided that their conduct is outweighed by the appropriate conduct of a sufficient number of others.[7] The structure of political institutions remains just and stable (for the right reasons) over time.

6. Some may think that the fact of reasonable pluralism means that the forms of fair adjudication among comprehensive doctrines must be only procedural and not substantive. This view is forcefully argued by Stuart Hampshire in *Innocence and Experience* (Cambridge, Mass.: Harvard University Press, 1989). In the text above, however, I assume that the several forms of liberalism are each substantive conceptions. For a thorough treatment of the issues, see the discussion by Joshua Cohen, "Pluralism and Proceduralism," *Chicago-Kent Law Review,* vol. 69, no. 3 (1994).

7. Liberal conceptions are also what we may call "liberalisms of freedom." Their three principles guarantee the basic rights and liberties, assign them a special priority, and assure to all citizens sufficient all-purpose means so that their freedoms are not purely formal. In this they stand with Kant, Hegel, and less obviously J. S. Mill. See further §7.3.

This idea of realistic utopia is importantly institutional. In the domestic case it connects with the way citizens conduct themselves under the institutions and practices within which they have grown up; in the international case with the way a people's character has historically developed. We depend on the facts of social conduct as historical knowledge and reflection establish them: for example, the facts that, historically, political and social unity do not depend on religious unity, and that well-ordered democratic peoples do not engage in war with one another. These observations and others will be essential as we proceed.

(v) Because religious, philosophical, or moral unity is neither possible nor necessary for social unity, if social stability is not merely a *modus vivendi*, it must be rooted in a reasonable political conception of right and justice affirmed by an overlapping consensus of comprehensive doctrines.

(vi) The political conception should have a reasonable idea of toleration derived entirely from ideas drawn from the category of the political.[8] This condition might not always be necessary, however, as we can think of cases when all the comprehensive doctrines held in society themselves provide for such a view. Nevertheless, the political conception will be strengthened if it contains a reasonable idea of toleration within itself, for that will show the reasonableness of toleration by public reason.

---

8. See *Political Liberalism*, pp. 60ff. The main points of this conception of toleration can be set out in summary fashion as follows: (1) Reasonable persons do not all affirm the same comprehensive doctrine. This is said to be a consequence of the "burdens of judgment." (2) Many reasonable doctrines are affirmed, not all of which can be true or right as judged from within any one comprehensive doctrine. (3) It is not unreasonable to affirm any one of the reasonable comprehensive doctrines. (4) Others who affirm reasonable doctrines different from ours are reasonable also. (5) In affirming our belief in a doctrine we recognize as reasonable, we are not being unreasonable. (6) Reasonable persons think it unreasonable to use political power, should they possess it, to repress other doctrines that are reasonable yet different from their own. These points may seem too narrow; for I recognize that every society also contains numerous unreasonable doctrines. In regard to this point, however, what is important to see is that how far unreasonable doctrines can be active and tolerated is not decided by what is said above, but by the principles of justice and the kinds of actions they permit. I am indebted to Erin Kelly for discussion of this point.

1.3. Parallel Conditions of Society of Peoples. Assuming that §1.2 above adequately indicates the conditions required for a reasonably just constitutional democracy, which I have called "a realistic utopia," what are the parallel conditions for a reasonably just Society of Peoples? This is too big a matter to discuss at this point in any detail. Yet it might be fruitful to note some of the parallels before we proceed, since doing so will foreshadow the argument to follow.

The first three conditions, I believe, are as strong in one case as in the other:

(i*) The reasonably just Society of well-ordered Peoples is *realistic* in the same ways as a liberal or decent domestic society. Here again we view peoples as they are (as organized within a reasonably just domestic society) and the Law of Peoples as it might be, that is, how it would be in a reasonably just Society of just and decent Peoples. The content of a reasonable Law of Peoples is ascertained by using the idea of the original position a second time with the parties now understood to be the representatives of peoples (§3). The idea of peoples rather than states is crucial at this point: it enables us to attribute moral motives— an allegiance to the principles of the Law of Peoples, which, for instance, permits wars only of self-defense—to peoples (as actors), which we cannot do for states (§2).[9]

The Law of Peoples is also realistic in a second way: it is workable and may be applied to ongoing cooperative political arrangements and relations between peoples. That this is the case cannot be shown until the content of the Law of Peoples is sketched (§4). For now, suffice it to say that the Law is expressed in the familiar terms of the freedom and equality of peoples, and it involves numerous jurisprudential and political (moral) ideas.

(ii*) A reasonably just Law of Peoples is *utopian* in that it uses political (moral) ideals, principles, and concepts to specify the reasonably

9. A question sure to be asked is: Why does the Law of Peoples use an original position at the second level that is fair to peoples and not to individual persons? What is it about peoples that gives them the status of the (moral) actors in the Law of Peoples? Part of the answer is given in §2, in which the idea of peoples is specified; but the fuller explanation is given in §11. Those who are troubled by this question should turn to it now.

right and just political and social arrangements for the Society of Peoples. In the domestic case, liberal conceptions of justice distinguish between the reasonable and the rational, and lie between altruism on one side and egoism on the other. The Law of Peoples duplicates these features. For example, we say (§2) that a people's interests are specified by their land and territory, their reasonably just political and social institutions, and their free civic culture with its many associations. These various interests ground the distinctions between the reasonable and the rational and show us how the relations among peoples may remain just and stable (for the right reasons) over time.

(iii*) A third condition requires that all the essential elements for a political conception of justice be contained within the category of the political. This condition will be satisfied for the Law of Peoples once we extend a liberal political conception for a constitutional democracy to the relations among peoples. Whether this extension can be carried out successfully has yet to be shown. But in any event, the extensions of the political always remain political, and comprehensive doctrines, religious, philosophical, and moral, always extend beyond it.

(iv*) The degree to which a reasonably just, effective institutional process enables members of different well-ordered societies to develop a sense of justice and support their government in honoring the Law of Peoples may differ from one society to another in the wider Society of Peoples. The fact of reasonable pluralism is more evident within a society of well-ordered peoples than it is within one society alone. An allegiance to the Law of Peoples need not be equally strong in all peoples, but it must be, ideally speaking, sufficient. I consider this question later in §15.5 under the heading of affinity, and I suggest there that the institutional process may be importantly weaker when allegiance to the Law of Peoples is also weaker.

This brings us to the remaining two conditions.

(v*) The unity of a reasonable Society of Peoples does not require religious unity. The Law of Peoples provides a content of public reason for the Society of Peoples parallel to the principles of justice in a democratic society.

(vi*) The argument for toleration derived from the idea of the reasonable holds equally in the wider Society of Peoples; the same reasoning applies in one case as in the other. The effect of extending a liberal conception of justice to the Society of Peoples, which encompasses many more religious and other comprehensive doctrines than any single people, makes it inevitable that, if member peoples employ public reason in their dealings with one another, toleration must follow.

These conditions are discussed in more detail as we proceed. How likely it is that such a Society of Peoples can exist is an important question, yet political liberalism asserts that the possibility is consistent with the natural order and with constitutions and laws as they might be. The idea of public reason[10] for the Society of Peoples is analogous to the idea of public reason in the domestic case when a shared basis of justification exists and can be uncovered by due reflection. Political liberalism, with its ideas of realistic utopia and public reason, denies what so much of political life suggests—that stability among peoples can never be more than a *modus vivendi*.

The idea of a reasonably just society of well-ordered peoples will not have an important place in a theory of international politics until such peoples exist and have learned to coordinate the actions of their governments in wider forms of political, economic, and social cooperation. When that happens, as I believe, following Kant, it will, the society of these peoples will form a group of satisfied peoples. As I shall maintain (§2), in view of their fundamental interests being satisfied, they will have no reason to go to war with one another. The familiar motives for war would be absent: such peoples do not seek to convert others to their religions, nor to conquer greater territory, nor to wield political power over another people. Through negotiation and trade they can fulfill their needs and economic interests. A detailed account of how and why all this takes shape over time will be an essential part of the theory of international politics.

1.4. Is Realistic Utopia a Fantasy? Some seem to think that this idea is a fantasy, particularly after Auschwitz. But why so? I wouldn't deny either the historical uniqueness of the Holocaust, or that it could

---

10. This idea is discussed in §7 of Part II. For the idea of public reason, see "The Idea of Public Reason Revisited" in this volume.

somewhere be repeated. Yet nowhere, other than German-occupied Europe between 1941 and 1945, has a charismatic dictator controlled the machinery of a powerful state so focused on carrying out the final and complete extermination of a particular people, hitherto regarded as members of society. The destruction of the Jews was carried out at great cost in men and equipment (use of railroads and the building of concentration camps, and much else) to the detriment of the desperate German war effort, especially during its last years. People of all ages, the elderly, children, and infants, were treated the same. Thus the Nazis pursued their aim to make German-occupied Europe *Judenrein* as an end in itself.[11]

Not to be overlooked is the fact that Hitler's demonic conception of the world was, in some perverse sense, religious. This is evident from its derivation and its leading ideas and hatreds. His "redemptive anti-semitism," as Saul Friedländer calls it, is one which includes not merely racial elements. "Redemptive anti-semitism," Friedländer writes, "is born from the fear of racial degeneration and the religious belief in redemption."[12] In Hitler's mind, a source of degeneration was intermarriage with Jews, which sullied the German bloodstream. In permitting this to happen, he thought, Germany was on the way to perdition. Redemption could come only with liberation from the Jews, with their expulsion from Europe, or, failing that, with their extermination. At the end of the second chapter of *Mein Kampf,* Hitler writes: "Today I be-

11. Here I draw on Raul Hilburg, *The Destruction of the European Jews,* 3 vols. (Chicago: University of Chicago Press, 1961), students' abbreviated edition in 1 vol. (New York: Holmes and Meier, 1985); and Hannah Arendt, *Eichmann in Jerusalem* (New York: Viking Press, 1963). For the source of Hitler's power, see Ian Kershaw, *The Hitler Myth: Image and Reality in the Third Reich* (New York: Oxford University Press, 1987), and Peter Fritzsche, *Germans into Nazis* (Cambridge, Mass.: Harvard University Press, 1998). See also Charles Maier, *The Unmasterable Past* (Cambridge, Mass.: Harvard University Press, 1988), especially pp. 80ff. Chapter 3 considers the question of the uniqueness of the Holocaust. See also Philippe Burrin, *Hitler and the Jews: Genesis of the Holocaust,* with an introduction by Saul Friedländer (London: Edward Arnold, 1994). Burrin believes that the Holocaust, with the aim of the final and complete extermination of the European Jews, begins roughly in September of 1941 with the increasing difficulties of the Russian campaign.

12. Saul Friedländer, *Nazi Germany and the Jews* (New York: HarperCollins, 1997), vol. 1, p. 87.

lieve that I am acting in accordance with the will of the Almighty Creator: by defending myself against the Jew I am fighting for the work of the Lord."[13]

The fact of the Holocaust and our now knowing that human society admits this demonic possibility, however, should not affect our hopes as expressed by the idea of a realistic utopia and Kant's *foedus pacificum*. Dreadful evils have long persisted. Since the time of the Emperor Constantine in the fourth century, Christianity punished heresy and tried to stamp out by persecution and religious wars what it regarded as false doctrine. To do so required the coercive powers of the state. The inquisition instituted by Pope Gregory IX was active throughout the Wars of Religion in the sixteenth and seventeenth centuries. In September of 1572, Pope Pius V went to the French Church of St. Louis in Rome where, joined by thirty-three Cardinals, he attended a Mass of thanksgiving to God for the religiously motivated massacre of fifteen thousand Protestant French Huguenots by Catholic factions on St. Bartholomew's Day that summer.[14] Heresy was widely regarded as worse than murder. This persecuting zeal has been the great curse of the Christian religion. It was shared by Luther and Calvin and the Protestant Reformers, and was not radically confronted in the Catholic Church until Vatican II.[15]

13. A police report has Hitler saying in 1926 in a speech in Munich: "Christmas was significant precisely for National Socialism, as Christ was the greatest precursor of the struggle against the Jewish world enemy. Christ had not been the Apostle of Peace that the Church afterward made of him, but rather the greatest fighting personality that ever lived. For millennia the teaching of Christ has been fundamental in the fight against the Jew as the enemy of humanity. The task that Christ has started, I will fulfill. National Socialism is nothing but the practical fulfillment of the teaching of Christ." See Friedländer, *Nazi Germany and the Jews*, p. 102.

14. Lord Acton, "The Massacre of St. Bartholomew," *North British Review* (October 1869). This description is from vol. II of Acton's *Collected Works* (Indianapolis: Liberty Classics, 1985), p. 227. It is noteworthy that at a ceremony in Paris, in August 1997, Pope John Paul II apologized for the church on the occasion of the anniversary of the massacre. See the *New York Times*, August 24, 1997, p. A3.

15. In the Council's *Declaration of Religious Freedom—Dignitatis Humanae* (1965), the Catholic Church committed itself to the principle of religious freedom as found in constitutional democracy. It declared the ethical doctrine of religious freedom resting on the dignity of the human person; a political doctrine with respect to the limits of government in religious matters; and a theological doctrine of the freedom of the

Were these evils greater or lesser than the Holocaust? We need not make such comparative judgments. Great evils are sufficient unto themselves. But the evils of the Inquisition and the Holocaust are not unrelated. Indeed, it seems clear that without Christian anti-semitism over many centuries—especially harsh in Russia and Eastern Europe—the Holocaust would not have happened.[16] That Hitler's "redemptive anti-semitism" strikes us as demonic madness—how could one believe such fantasies?—doesn't change this fact.

Yet we must not allow these great evils of the past and present to undermine our hope for the future of our society as belonging to a Society of liberal and decent Peoples around the world. Otherwise, the wrongful, evil, and demonic conduct of others destroys us too and seals their victory. Rather, we must support and strengthen our hope by developing a reasonable and workable conception of political right and justice applying to the relations between peoples. To accomplish this we may follow Kant's lead and begin from the political conception of a rea-

---

church in its relations to the political and social world. According to this declaration, all persons, whatever their faith, have the right of religious liberty on the same terms. As John Courtney Murray, S. J., said: "A longstanding ambiguity had finally been cleared up. The Church does not deal with the secular world in terms of a double standard—freedom for the Church when Catholics are in the minority—privilege for the Church and intolerance of others when Catholics are a majority." See the *Documents of Vatican II,* ed. Walter Abbott, S. J. (New York: American Press, 1966), p. 673.

16. In a radio address to the United States on April 4, 1933, the prominent Protestant clergyman Bishop Otto Dibelius defended the new German regime's April 1, 1933, boycott of the Jews (originally scheduled to last five days). In a confidential Easter message to the pastors in his province, he said: "My Dear Brethren! We all not only understand but are fully sympathetic to the recent motivations out of which the *völkisch* movement has emerged. Notwithstanding the evil sound the term has frequently acquired, I have always considered myself an anti-semite. One cannot ignore that Jewry has played a leading role in all the destructive manifestations of modern civilization." Dietrich Bonhoeffer, who later was to play a heroic role in the resistance and who became a leader of the Confessional Church, himself said in regard to the April Boycott: "In the Church of Christ, we have never lost sight of the idea that the 'Chosen People,' who nailed the Savior of the world to the cross, must bear the curse of the action through a long history of suffering." For both quotes see Friedländer, *Nazi Germany and the Jews,* pp. 42 and 45 respectively. It would stand to reason that in a decent society any such boycott organized by the state should be considered a blatant violation of freedom of religion and liberty of conscience. Why didn't these clergymen think so?

sonably just constitutional democracy that we have already formulated. We then proceed to extend that conception outward to the Society of liberal and decent Peoples (§4). Proceeding this way assumes the reasonableness of political liberalism; and developing a reasonable Law of Peoples out of political liberalism confirms its reasonableness. This Law is supported by the fundamental interests of constitutional democracies and other decent societies. No longer simply longing, our hope becomes reasonable hope.

§2. Why Peoples and Not States?

2.1. Basic Features of Peoples. This account of the Law of Peoples conceives of liberal democratic peoples (and decent peoples) as the actors in the Society of Peoples, just as citizens are the actors in domestic society. Starting from a political conception of society, political liberalism describes both citizens and peoples by political conceptions that specify their nature, a conception of citizens in one case, of peoples acting through their governments in the other. Liberal peoples have three basic features: a reasonably just constitutional democratic government that serves their fundamental interests; citizens united by what Mill called "common sympathies";[17] and finally, a moral nature. The first is institutional, the second is cultural, and the third requires

17. At this initial stage, I use the first sentences of chapter XVI of J. S. Mill's *Considerations* (1862) in which he uses an idea of nationality to describe a people's culture. He says: "A portion of mankind may be said to constitute a Nationality, if they are united among themselves by common sympathies, which do not exist between them and any others—which make them cooperate with each other more willingly than with other people, desire to be under the same government, and desire that it should be government by themselves, or a portion of themselves, exclusively. This feeling of nationality may have been generated by various causes. Sometimes it is the effect of identity of race and descent. Community of language, community of religion, greatly contribute to it. Geographical limits are one of its causes. But the strongest of all is identity of political antecedents; the possession of national history, and consequent community of recollections; collective pride and humiliation, pleasure and regret, connected with the same incidents in the past. None of these circumstances, however, are necessarily sufficient by themselves." *Considerations on Representative Government,* ed. J. M. Robson (Toronto: University of Toronto Press, 1977), in *Collected Works,* vol. XIX, chap. XVI, p. 546.

a firm attachment to a political (moral) conception of right and justice.[18]

By saying that a people have a reasonably just (though not necessarily a fully just) constitutional democratic government I mean that the government is effectively under their political and electoral control, and that it answers to and protects their fundamental interests as specified in a written or unwritten constitution and in its interpretation. The regime is not an autonomous agency pursuing its own bureaucratic ambitions. Moreover, it is not directed by the interests of large concentrations of private economic and corporate power veiled from public knowledge and almost entirely free from accountability. What institutions and practices might be necessary to keep a constitutional democratic government reasonably just, and to prevent it from being corrupted, is a large topic I cannot pursue here, beyond noting the truism that it is necessary to frame institutions in such a way as to motivate people sufficiently, both citizens and government officers, to honor them, and to remove the obvious temptations to corruption.[19]

As for a liberal people being united by common sympathies and a desire to be under the same democratic government, if those sympathies were entirely dependent upon a common language, history, and political culture, with a shared historical consciousness, this feature would rarely, if ever, be fully satisfied. Historical conquests and immigration have caused the intermingling of groups with different cultures and historical memories who now reside within the territory of most contemporary democratic governments. Notwithstanding, the Law of Peoples starts with the need for common sympathies, no matter what their source may be. My hope is that, if we begin in this simplified way,

18. I am much indebted to John Cooper for instructive discussion about these features.

19. An example worth mentioning is public financing of both elections and forums for public political discussion, without which sensible public politics is unlikely to flourish. When politicians are beholden to their constituents for essential campaign funds, and a very unequal distribution of income and wealth obtains in the background culture, with the great wealth being in the control of corporate economic power, is it any wonder that congressional legislation is, in effect, written by lobbyists, and Congress becomes a bargaining chamber in which laws are bought and sold?

we can work out political principles that will, in due course, enable us to deal with more difficult cases where all the citizens are not united by a common language and shared historical memories. One thought that encourages this way of proceeding is that within a reasonably just liberal (or decent) polity it is possible, I believe, to satisfy the reasonable cultural interests and needs of groups with diverse ethnic and national backgrounds. We proceed on the assumption that the political principles for a reasonably just constitutional regime allow us to deal with a great variety of cases, if not all.[20]

Finally, liberal peoples have a certain moral character. Like citizens in domestic society, liberal peoples are both reasonable and rational, and their rational conduct, as organized and expressed in their elections and votes, and the laws and policies of their government, is similarly constrained by their sense of what is reasonable. As reasonable citizens in domestic society offer to cooperate on fair terms with other citizens, so (reasonable) liberal (or decent) peoples offer fair terms of cooperation to other peoples. A people will honor these terms when assured that other peoples will do so as well. This leads us to the principles of political justice in the first case and the Law of Peoples in the other. It will be crucial to describe how this moral nature comes about and how it can be sustained from one generation to the next.

2.2. Peoples Lack Traditional Sovereignty. Another reason I use the term "peoples" is to distinguish my thinking from that about political states as traditionally conceived, with their powers of sovereignty included in the (positive) international law for the three centuries after the Thirty Years' War (1618–1648). These powers include the right to go to war in pursuit of state policies—Clausewitz's pursuit of politics by other means—with the ends of politics given by a state's rational prudential interests.[21] The powers of sovereignty also grant a state a

---

20. Here I think of the idea of nation as distinct from the idea of government or state, and I interpret it as referring to a pattern of cultural values of the kind described by Mill in note 17 above. In thinking of the idea of nation in this way I follow Yael Tamir's highly instructive *Liberal Nationalism* (Princeton: Princeton University Press, 1993).

21. It would be unfair to Clausewitz not to add that for him the state's interests can include regulative moral aims of whatever kind, and thus the aims of war may be to defend democratic societies against tyrannical regimes, somewhat as in World War II.

certain autonomy (discussed below) in dealing with its own people. From my perspective this autonomy is wrong.

In developing the Law of Peoples the first step is to work out the principles of justice for domestic society. Here the original position takes into account only persons contained within such a society, since we are not considering relations with other societies. That position views society as closed: persons enter only by birth, and exit only by death. There is no need for armed forces, and the question of the government's right to be prepared militarily does not arise and would be denied if it did. An army is not to be used against its own people. The principles of domestic justice allow a police force to keep domestic order and a judiciary and other institutions to maintain an orderly rule of law.[22] All this is very different from an army that is needed to defend against outlaw states. Although domestic principles of justice are consistent with a qualified right to war, they do not of themselves establish that right. The basis of that right depends on the Law of Peoples, still to be worked out. This law, as we shall see, will restrict a state's internal sovereignty or (political) autonomy, its alleged right to do as it wills with people within its own borders.

Thus, in working out the Law of Peoples, a government as the political organization of its people is not, as it were, the author of all of its own powers. The war powers of governments, whatever they might be, are only those acceptable within a reasonable Law of Peoples. Presuming the existence of a government whereby a people is domestically organized with institutions of background justice does not prejudge these questions. We must reformulate the powers of sovereignty

---

For him the aims of politics are not part of the theory of war, although they are ever-present and may properly affect the conduct of war. On this, see the instructive remarks of Peter Paret, "Clausewitz," in *The Makers of Modern Strategy,* ed. Peter Paret (Princeton: Princeton University Press, 1986), pp. 209–213. The view I have expressed in the text above characterizes the *raison d'état* as pursued by Frederick the Great. See Gerhard Ritter, *Frederick the Great,* trans. Peter Paret (Berkeley: University of California Press, 1968), chap. 10 and the statement on p. 197.

22. I stress here that the Law of Peoples does not question the legitimacy of government's authority to enforce the rule of democratic law. The supposed alternative to the government's so-called monopoly of power allows private violence for those with the will and the means to exercise it.

in light of a reasonable Law of Peoples and deny to states the traditional rights to war and to unrestricted internal autonomy.

Moreover, this reformulation accords with a recent dramatic shift in how many would like international law to be understood. Since World War II international law has become stricter. It tends to limit a state's right to wage war to instances of self-defense (also in the interests of collective security), and it also tends to restrict a state's right to internal sovereignty. The role of human rights connects most obviously with the latter change as part of the effort to provide a suitable definition of, and limits on, a government's internal sovereignty. At this point I leave aside the many difficulties of interpreting these rights and limits, and take their general meaning and tendency as clear enough. What is essential is that our elaboration of the Law of Peoples should fit these two basic changes, and give them a suitable rationale.[23]

The term "peoples," then, is meant to emphasize these singular features of peoples as distinct from states, as traditionally conceived, and to highlight their moral character and the reasonably just, or decent, nature of their regimes. It is significant that peoples' rights and duties in regard to their so-called sovereignty derive from the Law of Peoples itself, to which they would agree along with other peoples in suitable circumstances. As just or decent peoples, the reasons for their conduct accord with the corresponding principles. They are not moved solely by their prudent or rational pursuit interests, the so-called reasons of state.

2.3. Basic Features of States. The following remarks show that the character of a people in the Law of Peoples is different from the character of what I refer to as states. States are the actors in many theories of international politics about the causes of war and the preservation

23. Daniel Philpott in his "Revolutions in Sovereignty," Ph.D. dissertation (Harvard University, 1995), argues that the changes in the powers of sovereignty from one period to another arise from the changes that occur in peoples' ideas of right and just domestic government. Accepting this view as roughly correct, the explanation for the shift would seem to lie in the rise and acceptance of constitutional democratic regimes, their success in World Wars I and II, and the gradual loss of faith in Soviet communism.

of peace.[24] They are often seen as rational, anxiously concerned with their power—their capacity (military, economic, diplomatic) to influence other states—and always guided by their basic interests.[25] The typical view of international relations is fundamentally the same as it was in Thucydides' day and has not been transcended in modern times, when world politics is still marked by the struggles of states for power, prestige, and wealth in a condition of global anarchy.[26] How far states differ from peoples rests on how rationality, the concern with power, and a state's basic interests are filled in. If *rationality* excludes the *reasonable* (that is, if a state is moved by the aims it has and ignores the criterion of reciprocity in dealing with other societies); if a state's concern with power is predominant; and if its interests include such things as converting other societies to the state's religion, enlarging its empire and winning territory, gaining dynastic or imperial or national prestige and glory, and increasing its relative economic strength—then the difference between states and peoples is enormous.[27] Such inter-

24. See Robert Gilpin's *War and Change in World Politics* (Cambridge: Cambridge University Press, 1981), chap. 1, pp. 9–25. See also Robert Axelrod's *The Complexity of Cooperation* (Princeton: Princeton University Press, 1997), chap. 4, "Choosing Sides," with its account of the alignments of countries in World War II.

25. Lord Palmerston said: "England has no eternal friends, and no eternal enemies; only eternal interests." See Donald Kagan, *Origins of War and the Preservation of Peace* (New York: Doubleday, 1995), p. 144.

26. Gilpin's main thesis is that "the fundamental nature of international relations has not changed over the millennia. International relations continue to be a recurring struggle for wealth and power among independent actors in a state of anarchy. The history of Thucydides is as meaningful a guide to the behavior of states today as when it was written in the fifth century B.C." See Gilpin, *War and Change in World Politics*, p. 7. He presents his reasons for this thesis in chapter 6.

27. In his great *History of the Peloponnesian War*, trans. Rex Warner (London: Penguin Books, 1954), Thucydides tells the story of the fated self-destruction of the Greek city-states in the long war between Athens and Sparta. The history ends in midstream, as if it is broken off. Did Thucydides stop, or was he unable to finish? It is as if he said: "and so on . . ." The tale of folly has gone on long enough. What moves the city-states is what makes the increasing self-destruction inevitable. Listen to the Athenians' first speech to the Spartans: "We have done nothing extraordinary, contrary to human nature in accepting empire when it was offered to us, then refusing to give it up. Very powerful motives prevent us from doing so—security, honor and self-interest. And we were not the first to act this way, far from it. It was always the rule that the weaker should be subject to the stronger, and, besides, we consider that we are worthy of our

ests as these tend to put a state at odds with other states and peoples, and to threaten their safety and security, whether they are expansionist or not. The background conditions also threaten hegemonic war.[28]

A difference between liberal peoples and states is that just liberal peoples limit their basic interests as required by the reasonable. In contrast, the content of the interests of states does not allow them to be stable for the right reasons: that is, from firmly accepting and acting upon a just Law of Peoples. Liberal peoples do, however, have their fundamental interests as permitted by their conceptions of right and justice. They seek to protect their territory, to ensure the security and safety of their citizens, and to preserve their free political institutions and the liberties and free culture of their civil society.[29] Beyond these interests, a liberal people tries to assure reasonable justice for all its citizens and for all peoples; a liberal people can live with other peoples of like character in upholding justice and preserving peace. Any hope we have of reaching a realistic utopia rests on there being reasonable lib-

---

power. Up to the present moment you too used to think that we were; but now, after calculating your interests, you are beginning to talk in terms of right and wrong. Considerations of this kind have never turned people aside from opportunities of aggrandizement offered by superior strength. Those who really deserve praise are those who, while human enough to enjoy power, nevertheless pay more attention to justice than compelled to by their situation. Certainly we think that if anyone were in our position, it would be evident whether we act in moderation or not" (Book I: 76).

It is clear enough how the cycle of self-destruction goes. Thucydides thinks that, if the Athenians had followed Pericles' advice not to expand their empire as long as the war with Sparta and its allies lasted, they might well have won. But with the invasion of Melos and the folly of the Sicilian adventure urged on by Alcibiades' advice and persuasion, they were doomed to self-destruction. Napoleon is reputed to have said, commenting on his invasion of Russia: "Empires die of indigestion." But he wasn't candid with himself. Empires die of gluttony, of the ever-expanding craving for power. What makes peace among liberal democratic peoples possible is the internal nature of peoples as constitutional democracies and the resulting change of the motives of citizens. For the purposes of our story of the possibility of realistic utopia it is important to recognize that Athens was not a liberal democracy, though it may have thought of itself as such. It was an autocracy of the 35,000 male members of the assembly over the total population of about 300,000.

28. Gilpin, *War and Change in World Politics,* esp. chap. 5, discusses the features of hegemonic war.

29. See the reasoning in §14, where I discuss a liberal people's right to war in self-defense.

eral constitutional (and decent) regimes sufficiently established and effective to yield a viable Society of Peoples.

§3. Two Original Positions

3.1. Original Position as Model of Representation. This part describes the first step of ideal theory. Before beginning the extension of the liberal idea of the social contract to the Law of Peoples, let us note that the original position with a veil of ignorance is a model of representation for liberal societies.[30] In what I am now calling the first use of the original position, it models what we regard—you and I, here and now[31]—as fair and reasonable conditions for the parties, who are rational representatives of free and equal, reasonable and rational citizens, to specify fair terms of cooperation for regulating the basic structure of this society. Since the original position includes the veil of ignorance, it also models what we regard as appropriate restrictions on reasons for adopting a political conception of justice for that structure. Given these features, we conjecture that the conception of political justice the parties would select is the conception that you and I, here and now, would regard as reasonable and rational and supported by the best reasons. Whether our conjecture is borne out will depend on whether you and I, here and now, can, on due reflection, endorse the principles adopted. Even if the conjecture is intuitively plausible, there are different ways of interpreting the reasonable and the rational, and of specifying restrictions on reasons and explaining the primary goods. There is no *a priori* guarantee that we have matters right.

Here five features are essential: (1) the original position models[32] the parties as representing citizens fairly; (2) it models them as ra-

---

30. See the discussion of the original position and the veil of ignorance in *Political Liberalism,* I: §4.

31. Note: "you and I" are "here and now" citizens of the same liberal democratic society working out the liberal conception of justice in question.

32. What is modeled is a *relation,* in this case, the relation of the parties representing citizens. In the second original position at the second level, what is modeled is the relation of the parties representing peoples.

tional; and (3) it models them as selecting from among available principles of justice those to apply to the appropriate subject, in this case the basic structure. In addition, (4) the parties are modeled as making these selections for appropriate reasons, and (5) as selecting for reasons related to the fundamental interests of citizens as reasonable and rational. We check that these five conditions are satisfied by noting that citizens are indeed represented fairly (reasonably), in view of the symmetry (or the equality) of their representatives' situation in the original position.[33] Next, the parties are modeled as rational, in that their aim is to do the best they can for citizens whose basic interests they represent, as specified by the primary goods, which cover their basic needs as citizens. Finally, the parties decide for appropriate reasons, because the veil of ignorance prevents the parties from invoking inappropriate reasons, given the aim of representing citizens as free and equal persons.

I repeat here what I have said in *Political Liberalism,* since it is relevant below.[34] Not allowing the parties to know people's comprehensive doctrines is one way in which the veil of ignorance is thick as opposed to thin. Many have thought a thick veil of ignorance to be without justification and have queried its grounds, especially given the great significance of comprehensive doctrines, religious and nonreligious. Since we should justify features of the original position when we can, consider the following. Recall that we seek a political conception of justice for a democratic society, viewed as a system of fair cooperation among free and equal citizens who willingly accept, as politically autonomous, the publicly recognized principles of justice determining the fair terms of that cooperation. The society in question, however, is one in which there is a diversity of comprehensive doctrines, all perfectly reasonable. This is the fact of reasonable pluralism, as opposed to the fact of pluralism as such. Now if all citizens are freely to endorse the political conception of justice, that conception must be able to

33. The idea here follows the precept of similar cases: persons equal in all relevant respects are to be represented equally.

34. This paragraph restates a long footnote on pp. 24–25 of the 1996 paperback edition of *Political Liberalism.* This footnote draws on an essay by Wilfried Hinsch, to whom I am much indebted, presented by him at Bad Homburg, in July 1992.

gain the support of citizens who affirm different and opposing, though reasonable, comprehensive doctrines, in which case we have an overlapping consensus of reasonable doctrines. I suggest that we leave aside how people's comprehensive doctrines connect with the content of the political conception of justice and, instead, regard that content as arising from the various fundamental ideas drawn from the public political culture of a democratic society. Putting people's comprehensive doctrines behind the veil of ignorance enables us to find a political conception of justice that can be the focus of an overlapping consensus and thereby serve as a public basis of justification in a society marked by the fact of reasonable pluralism. None of what I am arguing here puts in question the description of a political conception of justice as a freestanding view, but it does mean that to explain the rationale of the thick veil of ignorance we must look to the fact of reasonable pluralism and the idea of an overlapping consensus of reasonable comprehensive doctrines.

3.2. Second Original Position as Model. At the next level, the idea of the original position is used again, but this time to extend a liberal conception to the Law of Peoples. As in the first instance, it is a model of representation, since it models what we would regard—you and I, here and now[35]—as fair conditions under which the parties, this time the rational representatives of liberal peoples, are to specify the Law of Peoples, guided by appropriate reasons. Both the parties as representatives and the peoples they represent are situated symmetrically and therefore fairly. In addition, peoples are modeled as rational, since the parties select from among available principles for the Law of Peoples guided by the fundamental interests of democratic societies, where these interests are expressed by the liberal principles of justice for a democratic society. Finally, the parties are subject to a veil of ignorance properly adjusted for the case at hand: they do not know, for example, the size of the territory, or the population, or the relative strength of the people whose fundamental interests they represent. Though they

35. In this case "you and I" are citizens of some liberal democratic society, but not of the same one.

do know that reasonably favorable conditions obtain that make constitutional democracy possible—since they know they represent liberal societies—they do not know the extent of their natural resources, or the level of their economic development, or other such information.

As members of societies well-ordered by liberal conceptions of justice, we conjecture that these features model what we would accept as fair—you and I, here and now—in specifying the basic terms of cooperation among peoples who, as liberal peoples, see themselves as free and equal. This makes the use of the original position at the second level a model of representation in exactly the same way it is at the first. Any differences are not in how the model of representation is used but in how it needs to be tailored given the agents modeled and the subject at hand.

Having said this, let us check that all five features are covered for the second original position. Thus, people's representatives are (1) reasonably and fairly situated as free and equal, and peoples are (2) modeled as rational. Also their representatives are (3) deliberating about the correct subject, in this case the content of the Law of Peoples. (Here we may view that law as governing the basic structure of the relations between peoples.) Moreover, (4) their deliberations proceed in terms of the right reasons (as restricted by a veil of ignorance). Finally, the selection of principles for the Law of Peoples is based (5) on a people's fundamental interests, given in this case by a liberal conception of justice (already selected in the first original position). Thus, the conjecture would appear to be sound in this case as in the first. But again there can be no guarantee.

Two questions, though, may arise. One is that in describing peoples as free and equal, and so as fairly and reasonably represented, it may appear that we have proceeded differently than in the domestic case. There we counted citizens as free and equal because that is how they conceive of themselves as citizens in a democratic society. Thus, they think of themselves as having the moral power to have a conception of the good, and to affirm or revise that conception if they so decide. They also see themselves as self-authenticating sources of claims, and capable of taking responsibility for their ends.[36] In the Law of Peoples

36. See *Political Liberalism*, pp. 29–35.

we do somewhat the same: we view *peoples* as conceiving of themselves as free and equal *peoples* in the Society of Peoples (according to the political conception of that society). This is parallel to, but not the same as, how in the domestic case the political conception determines the way citizens are to see themselves according to their moral powers and higher-order interests.

The second question involves another parallel to the domestic case. The original position denied to the representatives of citizens any knowledge of citizens' comprehensive conceptions of the good. That restriction called for a careful justification.[37] There is also a serious question in the present case. Why do we suppose that the representatives of liberal peoples ignore any knowledge of the people's comprehensive conception of the good? The answer is that a liberal society with a constitutional regime does not, *as a liberal society,* have a *comprehensive* conception of the good. Only the citizens and associations within the civic society in the domestic case have such conceptions.

3.3. Fundamental Interests of Peoples. In thinking of themselves as free and equal, how do peoples (in contrast to states) see themselves and their fundamental interests? These interests of liberal peoples are specified, I said (§2.3), by their reasonable conception of political justice. Thus, they strive to protect their political independence and their free culture with its civil liberties, to guarantee their security, territory, and the well-being of their citizens. Yet a further interest is also significant: applied to peoples, it falls under what Rousseau calls *amour-propre.*[38] This interest is a people's proper self-respect of themselves as a people, resting on their common awareness of their trials during their history and of their culture with its accomplishments. Altogether distinct from

37. See the long footnote on pp. 24–25 of the 1996 paperback edition of *Political Liberalism,* restated above.

38. My account here follows N. J. H. Dent in his *Rousseau* (Oxford: Basil Blackwell, 1988) and Frederick Neuhouser's essay "Freedom and the General Will," *Philosophical Review,* July 1993. Donald Kagan in his *Origins of War and the Preservation of Peace* notes two meanings of honor. As I describe them in the text (above and in the next section), one is compatible with satisfied peoples and their stable peace, whereas the other is not, setting the stage for conflict. I believe Kagan underestimates the great difference between the two meanings of honor.

their self-concern for their security and the safety of their territory, this interest shows itself in a people's insisting on receiving from other peoples a proper respect and recognition of their equality. What distinguishes peoples from states—and this is crucial—is that just peoples are fully prepared to grant the very same proper respect and recognition to other peoples as equals. Their equality doesn't mean, however, that inequalities of certain kinds are not agreed to in various cooperative institutions among peoples, such as the United Nations, ideally conceived. This recognition of inequalities, rather, parallels citizens' accepting functional social and economic inequalities in their liberal society.

It is, therefore, part of a people's being reasonable and rational that they are ready to offer to other peoples fair terms of political and social cooperation. These fair terms are those that a people sincerely believes other equal peoples might accept also; and should they do so, a people will honor the terms it has proposed even in those cases where that people might profit by violating them.[39] Thus, the criterion of reciprocity applies to the Law of Peoples in the same way it does to the principles of justice for a constitutional regime. This reasonable sense of due respect, willingly accorded to other reasonable peoples, is an essential element of the idea of peoples who are satisfied with the status quo for the right reasons. It is compatible with ongoing cooperation among them over time and the mutual acceptance and adherence to the Law of Peoples. Part of the answer to political realism is that this reasonable sense of proper respect is not unrealistic, but is itself the outcome of democratic domestic institutions. I will come back to this argument later.

§4. The Principles of the Law of Peoples

4.1. Statement of the Principles. Initially, we may assume that the outcome of working out the Law of Peoples only for liberal democratic societies will be the adoption of certain familiar principles of

---

39. This account parallels the idea of the reasonable used in a liberal society. See *Political Liberalism*, II: §1.

equality among peoples. These principles will also, I assume, make room for various forms of cooperative associations and federations among peoples, but will not affirm a world-state. Here I follow Kant's lead in *Perpetual Peace* (1795) in thinking that a world government— by which I mean a unified political regime with the legal powers normally exercised by central governments—would either be a global despotism or else would rule over a fragile empire torn by frequent civil strife as various regions and peoples tried to gain their political freedom and autonomy.[40] As I discuss below, it may turn out that there will be many different kinds of organizations subject to the judgment of the Law of Peoples and charged with regulating cooperation among them and meeting certain recognized duties. Some of these organizations (such as the United Nations ideally conceived) may have the authority to express for the society of well-ordered peoples their condemnation of unjust domestic institutions in other countries and clear cases of the violation of human rights. In grave cases they may try to correct them by economic sanctions, or even by military intervention. The scope of these powers covers all peoples and reaches their domestic affairs.

These large conclusions call for some discussion. Proceeding in a way analogous to the procedure in *A Theory of Justice*,[41] let's look first

40. Kant says in Ak:VIII:367: "The idea of international law presupposes the separate existence of independent neighboring states. Although this condition is itself a state of war (unless federative union prevents the outbreak of hostilities), this is rationally preferable to the amalgamation of states under one superior power, as this would end in one universal monarchy, and laws always lose in vigor what government gains in extent; hence a condition of soulless despotism falls into anarchy after stifling seeds of good." Kant's attitude to universal monarchy was shared by other writers of the eighteenth century. See, for example, Hume's "Of the Balance of Power" (1752), in *Political Essays,* ed. K. Haakonssen (Cambridge: Cambridge University Press, 1994). F. H. Hinsley, *Power and the Pursuit of Peace* (Cambridge: Cambridge University Press, 1966), also mentions Montesquieu, Voltaire, and Gibbon, pp. 162ff., and he has an instructive discussion of Kant's ideas in chapter 4. See also Patrick Riley, *Kant's Political Philosophy* (Totowa, N.J.: Rowman and Littlefield, 1983), chaps. 5 and 6.

41. See *A Theory of Justice,* where chapter 2 discusses the principles of justice and chapter 3 gives the reasoning from the original position concerning the selection of principles. All references to *A Theory of Justice* are to the original edition (Harvard University Press, 1971).

at familiar and traditional principles of justice among free and democratic peoples:[42]

1. Peoples are free and independent, and their freedom and independence are to be respected by other peoples.
2. Peoples are to observe treaties and undertakings.
3. Peoples are equal and are parties to the agreements that bind them.
4. Peoples are to observe a duty of non-intervention.
5. Peoples have the right of self-defense but no right to instigate war for reasons other than self-defense.
6. Peoples are to honor human rights.
7. Peoples are to observe certain specified restrictions in the conduct of war.
8. Peoples have a duty to assist other peoples living under unfavorable conditions that prevent their having a just or decent political and social regime.[43]

4.2. Comments and Qualifications. This statement of principles is, admittedly, incomplete. Other principles need to be added, and the principles listed require much explanation and interpretation. Some are superfluous in a society of well-ordered peoples, for example, the seventh regarding the conduct of war and the sixth regarding human rights. Yet the main point is that free and independent well-ordered peoples are ready to recognize certain basic principles of political justice as governing their conduct. These principles constitute the basic charter of the Law of Peoples. A principle such as the fourth—that of non-intervention—will obviously have to be qualified in the general case of outlaw states and grave violations of human rights. Although suitable for a society of well-ordered peoples, it fails in the case of a so-

---

42. See J. L. Brierly, *The Law of Nations: An Introduction to the Law of Peace,* 6th ed. (Oxford: Clarendon Press, 1963), and Terry Nardin, *Law, Morality, and the Relations of States* (Princeton: Princeton University Press, 1983). Both Brierly and Nardin give similar lists as principles of international law.

43. This principle is especially controversial. I discuss it in §§15–16.

ciety of disordered peoples in which wars and serious violations of human rights are endemic.

The right to independence, and equally the right to self-determination, hold only within certain limits, yet to be specified by the Law of Peoples for the general case.[44] Thus, no people has the right to self-determination, or a right to secession, at the expense of subjugating another people.[45] Nor may a people protest their condemnation by the world society when their domestic institutions violate human rights, or limit the rights of minorities living among them. A people's right to independence and self-determination is no shield from that condemnation, nor even from coercive intervention by other peoples in grave cases.

There will also be principles for forming and regulating federations (associations) of peoples, and standards of fairness for trade and other cooperative institutions.[46] Certain provisions will be included for mutual assistance among peoples in times of famine and drought and, insofar as it is possible, provisions for ensuring that in all reasonable liberal (and decent) societies people's basic needs are met.[47] These provisions will specify duties of assistance (see §15) in certain situations, and they will vary in stringency with the severity of the case.

4.3. Role of Boundaries. An important role of a people's government, however arbitrary a society's boundaries may appear from a historical point of view, is to be the representative and effective agent of a people as they take responsibility for their territory and its environmental in-

---

44. Charles Beitz, *Political Theory and International Relations* (Princeton: Princeton University Press, 1979), chap. 2, has a valuable discussion of the question of the autonomy of states, with a summary of the main points on pp. 121–123. I owe much to his account.

45. A clear example regarding secession is whether the South had a right to secede in 1860–1861. On my account it had no such right, since it seceded to perpetuate its domestic institution of slavery. This was as severe a violation of human rights as any, and it extended to nearly half the population.

46. On these principles, see Robert Keohane, *After Hegemony* (Princeton: Princeton University Press, 1984).

47. By basic needs I mean roughly those that must be met if citizens are to be in a position to take advantage of the rights, liberties, and opportunities of their society. These needs include economic means as well as institutional rights and freedoms.

tegrity, as well as for the size of their population. As I see it the point of the institution of property is that, unless a definite agent is given responsibility for maintaining an asset and bears the loss for not doing so, that asset tends to deteriorate. In this case the asset is the people's territory and its capacity to support them *in perpetuity;* and the agent is the people themselves as politically organized. As I noted in the Introduction, they are to recognize that they cannot make up for their irresponsibility in caring for their land and its natural resources by conquest in war or by migrating into other people's territory without their consent.[48]

It does not follow from the fact that boundaries are historically arbitrary that their role in the Law of Peoples cannot be justified. On the contrary, to fix on their arbitrariness is to fix on the wrong thing. In the absence of a world-state, there *must* be boundaries of some kind, which when viewed in isolation will seem arbitrary, and depend to some degree on historical circumstances. In a reasonably just (or at least decent) Society of Peoples, the inequalities of power and wealth are to be decided by all peoples for themselves. How all this works out in my account—an essential feature of a realistic utopia—must wait until §§15 and 16, where I discuss the duty of assistance that reasonably just liberal peoples and decent peoples owe to societies burdened by unfavorable conditions.

4.4. Argument in Second Original Position. A large part of the argument in the original position in the domestic case concerns selecting among the various formulations of the two principles of justice (when the view adopted is liberal), and between liberal principles and such

48. This remark implies that a people has at least a qualified right to limit immigration. I leave aside here what these qualifications might be. There are also important assumptions I make here which are not considered until Part III, §15, where I examine the duties of well-ordered societies to those societies burdened by unfavorable conditions. Another reason for limiting immigration is to protect a people's political culture and its constitutional principles. See Michael Walzer, *Spheres of Justice* (New York: Basic Books, 1983), pp. 38ff. for a good statement. He says on page 39: "To tear down the walls of the state is not, as Sidgwick worriedly suggested, to create a world without walls, but rather to create a thousand petty fortresses. The fortresses, too, can be torn down: all that is necessary is a global state sufficiently powerful to overwhelm the local communities. Then the result would be the world of the political economist, as Sidgwick described it [or of global capitalism, I might add]—a world of deracinated men and women."

alternatives as the classical, or the average, principle of utilitarianism, and various forms of rational intuitionism and moral perfectionism.[49] By contrast, the only alternatives for the parties to pick from in the second-level original position are formulations of the Law of Peoples. Three main ways in which the first and the second use of the original position are not analogous are these:

(1) A people of a constitutional democracy has, as a *liberal* people, no *comprehensive* doctrine of the good (§3.2 above), whereas individual citizens within a liberal domestic society do have such conceptions, and to deal with their needs as citizens, the idea of primary goods is used.

(2) A people's fundamental interests as a people are specified by its political conception of justice and the principles in the light of which they agree to the Law of Peoples, whereas citizens' fundamental interests are given by their conception of the good and their realizing to an adequate degree their two moral powers.

(3) The parties in the second original position select among different formulations or interpretations of the eight principles of the Law of Peoples, as illustrated by the reasons mentioned for the restrictions of the two powers of sovereignty (§2.2).

Part of the versatility of the original position is displayed in how it is used in the two cases. These differences between the two cases depend importantly on how, in each instance, the parties are understood.

The parties' first task in the second original position is to specify the Law of Peoples—its ideals, principles, and standards—and how those norms apply to political relations among peoples. If a reasonable pluralism of comprehensive doctrines is a basic feature of a constitutional democracy with its free institutions, we may assume that there is an even greater diversity in the comprehensive doctrines affirmed among the members of the Society of Peoples with its many different cultures and traditions. Hence a classical, or average, utilitarian principle would not be accepted by peoples, since no people organized by its government is prepared to count, *as a first principle,* the benefits for another people as outweighing the hardships imposed on itself. Well-ordered peoples insist on an *equality* among themselves as peoples, and this insistence rules out any form of the principle of utility.

---

49. See *A Theory of Justice,* chapters 2 and 3.

I contend that the eight principles of the Law of Peoples (see §4.1) are superior to any others. Much as in examining the distributive principles in justice as fairness, we begin with the baseline of equality—in the case of justice as fairness the equality of social and economic primary goods, in this case the equality of and the equal rights of all peoples. In the first case we asked whether any departure from the baseline of equality would be agreed to provided that it is to the benefit of all citizens of society and, in particular, the least advantaged. (I only hint here at the reasoning.) With the Law of Peoples, however, persons are not under one but many governments, and the representatives of peoples will want to preserve the equality and independence of their own society. In the working of organizations and loose[50] confederations of peoples, inequalities are designed to serve the many ends that peoples share. In this case the larger and smaller peoples will be ready to make larger and smaller contributions and to accept proportionately larger and smaller returns.

Thus, in the argument in the original position at the second level I consider the merits of only the eight principles of the Law of Peoples listed in §4.1. These familiar and largely traditional principles I take from the history and usages of international law and practice. The parties are not given a menu of alternative principles and ideals from which to select, as they are in *Political Liberalism*, or in *A Theory of Justice*. Rather, the representatives of well-ordered peoples simply reflect on the advantages of these principles of equality among peoples and see no reason to depart from them or to propose alternatives. These principles must, of course, satisfy the criterion of reciprocity, since this criterion holds at both levels—both between citizens as citizens and peoples as peoples.

Certainly we could imagine alternatives. For example: principle (5) has the obvious alternative, long supported by the practice of European states in modern history, that a state may go to war in the rational pursuit of its own interests. These may be religious, dynastic, territorial, or the glory of conquest and empire. In view of the account below of democratic peace (§5), however, that alternative would be rejected

---

50. I use this adjective to emphasize that confederations are much less tight than federations and do not involve the powers of federal governments.

by liberal peoples. As shown later, it would also be rejected by decent peoples (§8.4).

The discussion in §2 of the two traditional powers of sovereignty brings out that the eight principles are open to different interpretations. It is these *interpretations,* of which there are many, that are to be debated in the second-level original position. Regarding the two powers of sovereignty, we ask: What kind of political norms do liberal peoples, given their fundamental interests, hope to establish to govern mutual relations both among themselves and with nonliberal peoples? Or what moral climate and political atmosphere do they wish to see in a reasonably just Society of well-ordered Peoples? In view of those fundamental interests, liberal peoples limit a state's right to engage in war to wars of self-defense (thus allowing collective security), and their concern for human rights leads them to limit a state's right of internal sovereignty. In the Law of Peoples the many difficulties of interpreting the eight principles I have listed take the place of the arguments for first principles in the domestic case. The problem of how to interpret these principles can always be raised and is to be debated from the point of view of the second-level original position.

4.5. Cooperative Organizations. In addition to agreeing to the principles that define the basic equality of all peoples, the parties will formulate guidelines for setting up cooperative organizations and agree to standards of fairness for trade as well as certain provisions for mutual assistance. Suppose there are three such organizations: one framed to ensure fair trade among peoples; another to allow a people to borrow from a cooperative banking system; and the third an organization with a role similar to that of the United Nations, which I will now refer to as a Confederation of Peoples (not states).[51]

Consider fair trade: suppose that liberal peoples assume that, when suitably regulated by a fair background framework,[52] a free competi-

51. Think of the first two organizations as in some ways analogous to GATT and the World Bank.

52. Here I assume, as in the domestic case, that, unless fair background conditions exist and are maintained over time from one generation to the next, market transactions will not remain fair, and unjustified inequalities among peoples will gradually develop. These background conditions and all that they involve have a role analogous to that of the basic structure in domestic society.

tive-market trading scheme is to everyone's mutual advantage, at least in the longer run. A further assumption here is that the larger nations with the wealthier economies will not attempt to monopolize the market, or to conspire to form a cartel, or to act as an oligopoly. With these assumptions, and supposing as before that the veil of ignorance holds, so that no people knows whether its economy is large or small, all would agree to fair standards of trade to keep the market free and competitive (when such standards can be specified, followed, and enforced). Should these cooperative organizations have unjustified distributive effects between peoples, these would have to be corrected, and taken into account by the duty of assistance, which I discuss later in §§15–16.

The two further cases of agreeing to a central bank and to a Confederation of Peoples can be treated in the same way. Always the veil of ignorance holds, and the organizations are mutually beneficial and are open to liberal democratic peoples free to make use of them on their own initiative. As in the domestic case, peoples think it reasonable to accept various functional inequalities once the baseline of equality is firmly established. Thus, depending on their size, some will make larger contributions to the cooperative bank than others (suitable interest being due on loans) and will pay larger dues in the organization of the Confederation of Peoples.[53]

53. What does the Law of Peoples say about the following situation? Suppose that two or more of the liberal democratic societies of Europe, say Belgium and the Netherlands, or these two together with France and Germany, decide they want to join and form a single society, or a single federal union. Assuming they are all liberal societies, any such union must be agreed to by an election in which in each society the decision whether to unite is thoroughly discussed. Moreover, since these societies are liberal, they adopt a liberal political conception of justice, which has the three characteristic kinds of principles, as well as satisfying the criterion of reciprocity, as all liberal conceptions of justice must do (§1.2). Beyond this condition, the electorate of these societies must vote on which political conception they believe to be the *most* reasonable, although all such conceptions are at least reasonable. A voter in such an election might vote for the difference principle (the most egalitarian liberal conception), should he or she think it is the most reasonable. Yet so long as the criterion of reciprocity is satisfied, other variants of the three characteristic principles are consistent with political liberalism. To avoid confusion, I add that what I later call the "duty of assistance" applies only to the duty that liberal and decent peoples have to assist *burdened* societies (§15). As I explain there, such societies are neither liberal nor decent.

§5. Democratic Peace and Its Stability

5.1. Two Kinds of Stability. To complete this overview of the Law of Peoples for well-ordered liberal societies, I must do two things. One is to distinguish two kinds of stability: stability for the right reasons and stability as a balance of forces. The other is to offer a reply to political realism as a theory of international politics, and to those who say that the idea of a realistic utopia among peoples is quixotic. I do so by sketching a view of democratic peace, from which follows a different view of war.

Consider first the two kinds of stability. Recall (from §1.2) that, in the domestic case, I mentioned a process whereby citizens develop a sense of justice as they grow up and take part in their just social world. As a realistically utopian idea, the Law of Peoples must have a parallel process that leads peoples, including both liberal and decent societies, to accept willingly and to act upon the legal norms embodied in a just Law of Peoples. This process is similar to that in the domestic case. Thus, when the Law of Peoples is honored by peoples over a certain period of time, with the evident intention to comply, and these intentions are mutually recognized, these peoples tend to develop mutual trust and confidence in one another. Moreover, peoples see those norms as advantageous for themselves and for those they care for, and therefore as time goes on they tend to accept that law as an ideal of conduct.[54] Without such a psychological process, which I shall call moral learning, the idea of realistic utopia for the Law of Peoples lacks an essential element.

As I have said, peoples (as opposed to states) have a definite moral nature (§2.1). This nature includes a certain proper pride and sense of honor; they may be proud of their history and achievements, as a *proper patriotism* allows. Yet the due respect they ask for is a due respect consistent with the equality of all peoples. Peoples must have interests—otherwise they would be either inert and passive, or likely to be swayed by unreasonable and sometimes blind passions and impulses. The interests which move peoples (and which distinguish them

54. The process here is similar to the gradual, if at first reluctant, acceptance of a principle of toleration.

from states) are reasonable interests guided by and congruent with a fair equality and a due respect for all peoples. As I will note later, it is these reasonable interests that make democratic peace possible, and the lack thereof causes peace between states to be at best a *modus vivendi,* a stable balance of forces only for the time being.

Recall that, in the domestic case, in adopting the principles for a conception of political right and justice, the parties must ask whether in a liberal society those principles are likely to be stable for the right reasons. Stability for the right reasons describes a situation in which, over the course of time, citizens acquire a sense of justice that inclines them not only to accept but to act upon the principles of justice. The selection of principles by the parties in the original position is always to be preceded by a careful consideration of whether the psychology of learning by citizens in well-ordered liberal societies leads them to acquire a sense of justice and a disposition to act from those principles.

Similarly, once the second original position argument is complete and includes the account of moral learning, we conjecture, first, that the Law of Peoples the parties would adopt is the law that we—you and I, here and now—would accept as fair in specifying the basic terms of cooperation among peoples. We also conjecture, second, that the just society of liberal peoples would be stable for the right reasons, meaning that its stability is not a mere *modus vivendi* but rests in part on an allegiance to the Law of Peoples itself.

Yet plainly, this second conjecture needs to be confirmed by what actually happens historically. The society of liberal peoples must in fact turn out to be stable with respect to the distribution of success among them. Here success refers not to a society's military prowess or the lack of it, but to other kinds of success: achievement of political and social justice for all its citizens, securing their basic freedoms, the fullness and expressiveness of the society's civic culture, as well as the decent economic well-being of all its people. Since the society of liberal peoples is stable for the right reasons, it is stable with respect to justice; and the institutions and practices among peoples continue to satisfy the relevant principles of right and justice, even though their relations and success are continually changing in view of political, economic, and social trends.

5.2. Reply to Realist Theory. I reply to the realist theory that international relations have not changed since Thucydides' day and that they continue to be an ongoing struggle for wealth and power[55] by recalling a familiar view of peace for a society of liberal peoples. It leads to a different view of war than the hegemonic theory of the realist.

The idea of a liberal democratic peace unites at least two ideas. One is the idea that between the unalterable miseries of life such as plagues and epidemics, on the one hand, and remote unchangeable causes such as fate and the will of God, on the other, there are political and social institutions that can be changed by the people. This idea led to the movement toward democracy in the eighteenth century. As Saint-Just said, "The idea of happiness is new in Europe."[56] What he meant was that the social order was no longer viewed as fixed: political and social institutions could be revised and reformed for the purpose of making peoples happier and more satisfied.

The other idea is that of the *moeurs douces* of Montesquieu,[57] the idea that a commercial society tends to fashion in its citizens certain virtues such as assiduity, industriousness, punctuality, and probity; and that commerce tends to lead to peace. Putting these two ideas together—that social institutions can be revised to make people more satisfied and happy (through democracy), and that commerce tends to lead to peace—we might surmise that democratic peoples engaged in commerce would tend not to have occasion to go to war with one another. Among other reasons, this is because what they lacked in commodities they could acquire more easily and cheaply by trade; and because, being liberal constitutional democracies, they would not be moved to try to convert other peoples to a state religion or other ruling comprehensive doctrine.

Recall the features of liberal societies (§2.1). They are, we have said,

55. See note 27 above.

56. See Albert Hirschman's *Rival Views of Market Society* (Cambridge, Mass.: Harvard University Press, 1992), pp. 105ff.

57. See Hirschman, *Rival Views,* pp. 107ff. The phrase *moeurs douces* (gentle manners) is in Montesquieu's *The Spirit of Laws,* trans. and ed. Anne Cohler, Basia Miller, and Harold Stone (Cambridge: Cambridge University Press, 1989), book 20, p. 338. In chapter 2 of that book, Montesquieu argues that commerce tends to lead to peace.

satisfied peoples, to use Raymond Aron's term.[58] Their basic needs are met, and their fundamental interests are fully compatible with those of other democratic peoples. (To call a people satisfied, by the way, doesn't mean that citizens of the society are necessarily cheerful and happy.) There is true peace among them because all societies are satisfied with the status quo for the right reasons.

Aron calls such a state of peace "peace by satisfaction" (as opposed to "peace by power" or "peace by impotence"), and he describes the conditions, in the abstract, necessary for it to obtain. He argues that political units must seek neither to extend their territory nor to rule over other populations. They must not seek to extend themselves, either to increase their material or human resources, to disseminate their institutions, or to enjoy the intoxicating pride of ruling.

I agree with Aron that these conditions are necessary to a lasting peace, and I argue that they would be fulfilled by peoples living under liberal constitutional democracies. These peoples honor a shared principle of legitimate government and are not swayed by the passion for power and glory, or the intoxicating pride of ruling. These passions may move a nobility and lesser aristocracy to earn their social standing and place in the sun; yet this class, or caste rather, does not have power in a constitutional regime. Such regimes are not bent on the religious conversion of other societies, since liberal peoples by their constitution have no state religion—they are not confessional states—even if their citizens are highly religious, individually or together in associations. Domination and striving for glory, the excitement of conquest and the pleasure of exercising power over others, do not move them against other peoples. All being satisfied in this way, liberal peoples have nothing to go to war about.

Moreover, liberal peoples are not inflamed by what Rousseau diagnosed as arrogant or wounded pride or by lack of due self-respect. Their self-respect rests on the freedom and integrity of their citizens and the justice and decency of their domestic political and social institutions. It rests also on the achievements of their public and civic

58. In this and the following paragraphs I draw on Raymond Aron's treatise, *Peace and War,* trans. R. Howard and A. B. Fox (Garden City: Doubleday, 1966), pp. 160ff.

culture. All these things are rooted in their civic society and make no essential reference to their being superior or inferior to other peoples. They mutually respect one another and recognize equality among peoples as consistent with that respect.

Aron also says that peace by satisfaction will be lasting only if it is general, that is, if it holds among all societies; otherwise there will be a return to competition for superior strength and an ultimate breakdown of peace. One strong state possessed of military and economic power and embarked on expansion and glory is sufficient to perpetuate the cycle of war and preparation for war. So once the idea of a world state is given up (§4.1), liberal and decent peoples' acceptance of the Law of Peoples is not alone sufficient. The Society of Peoples needs to develop new institutions and practices under the Law of Peoples to constrain outlaw states when they appear. Among these new practices should be the promotion of human rights: it should be a fixed concern of the foreign policy of all just and decent regimes.[59]

The idea of democratic peace implies that, when liberal peoples do go to war, it is only with unsatisfied societies, or outlaw states (as I have called them). This they do when such a state's policies threaten their security and safety, since they must defend the freedom and independence of their liberal culture and oppose states that strive to subject and dominate them.[60]

5.3. More Precise Idea of Democratic Peace. The possibility of democratic peace is not incompatible with *actual* democracies—being marked, as they are, by considerable injustice, oligarchic tendencies, and monopolistic interests—intervening, often covertly, in smaller or weaker countries, and even in less well-established and secure democ-

---

59. In Part III, §15 I note that insistence on the protection of human rights may put pressure on a society to move toward a constitutional regime, for example, if such a regime is necessary for the prevention of famine and starvation.

60. Add also when they are harshly pressured by a state to accept oppressive terms of accommodation that are so unreasonable that no self-respecting liberal people affirming the liberty of its culture could reasonably be expected to accept them. An illustrative example is Germany's presumptive demand to France before the outbreak of World War I. On this example see Kagan, *Origins of War and the Preservation of Peace,* p. 202.

racies. But to prove as much, the idea of a democratic peace needs to be made more precise; and I shall formulate a guiding hypothesis to express its meaning.

(1) To the extent that each of the reasonably just constitutional democratic societies fully satisfies the five features (briefly described below) of such a regime—and its citizens understand and accept its political institutions with their history and achievements—the peace among them is made more secure.

(2) To the extent that each of the liberal societies fully satisfies the conditions described in (1) above, all are less likely to engage in war with nonliberal outlaw states, except on grounds of legitimate self-defense (or in the defense of their legitimate allies), or intervention in severe cases to protect human rights.

A reasonably just constitutional democratic society, to review, is one that combines and orders the two basic values of liberty and equality in terms of three characteristic principles (§1.2). The first two specify basic rights, liberties, and opportunities, and assign to these freedoms a priority characteristic of such a regime. The third principle is the assurance of sufficient all-purpose means to enable all citizens to make intelligent and effective use of their freedoms. This third feature must satisfy the criterion of reciprocity, and it requires a basic structure that prevents social and economic inequalities from becoming excessive. Without institutions (a) to (e) below, or similar arrangements, such excessive and unreasonable inequalities tend to develop.

The guaranteed constitutional liberties taken alone are properly criticized as purely formal.[61] By themselves, without the third characteristic principle above, they are an impoverished form of liberalism—indeed not liberalism at all but libertarianism.[62] The latter does not combine liberty and equality in the way liberalism does; it lacks the criterion of reciprocity and allows excessive social and economic inequalities as judged by that criterion. A libertarian regime would not

61. See *Political Liberalism,* VII: §3 and VIII: §7.
62. Ibid., VII: §3.

have stability for the right reasons, which is always lacking in a purely formal constitutional regime. Important requirements to achieve that stability are these:

(a) A certain fair equality of opportunity, especially in education and training. (Otherwise all parts of society cannot take part in the debates of public reason or contribute to social and economic policies.)

(b) A decent distribution of income and wealth meeting the third condition of liberalism: all citizens must be assured the all-purpose means necessary for them to take intelligent and effective advantage of their basic freedoms. (In the absence of this condition, those with wealth and income tend to dominate those with less and increasingly to control political power in their own favor.)

(c) Society as employer of last resort through general or local government, or other social and economic policies. (The lack of a sense of long-term security and of the opportunity for meaningful work and occupation is destructive not only of citizens' self-respect, but of their sense that they are members of society and not simply caught in it.)

(d) Basic health care assured for all citizens.

(e) Public financing of elections and ways of assuring the availability of public information on matters of policy.[63] (A statement of the need for these arrangements merely hints at what is needed both to ensure that representatives and other officials are sufficiently independent of particular social and economic interests and to provide the knowledge and information upon which policies can be formed and intelligently assessed by citizens.)

These requirements are satisfied by the principles of justice of all liberal conceptions. They cover essential prerequisites for a basic structure within which the ideal of public reason, when conscientiously fol-

63. Ibid., VIII: §§12–13.

lowed by citizens, may protect the basic liberties and prevent social and economic inequalities from becoming excessive. Since the ideal of public reason contains a form of public political deliberation, these conditions, most clearly the first three, are necessary for this deliberation to be possible and fruitful. A belief in the importance of public deliberation is vital for a reasonable constitutional regime, and specific arrangements need to be laid down to support and encourage it.

Much more would need to be said to sharpen the hypothesis of democratic peace, for many important questions remain. For example, to what degree must each of the requirements (a) through (e) be institutionalized? What are the consequences when some of them are weak while others are strong? How do they work together? Then there are comparison questions: for example, how important is public financing of elections in comparison with, say, fair equality of opportunity? It would be difficult even to guess at definitive answers to these questions, as this would require much background and information. Yet history may enlighten us about much that we want to know. The essential point is that, to the extent that constitutional democratic peoples have the features (a) through (e), their conduct supports the idea of a democratic peace.

5.4. Democratic Peace Seen in History. The historical record seems to suggest that stability for the right reasons would be satisfied in a society of reasonably just constitutional democracies. Though liberal democratic societies have often engaged in war against nondemocratic states,[64] since 1800 firmly established liberal societies have not fought one another.[65]

---

64. See Jack S. Levy, "Domestic Politics and War," in *The Origin and Prevention of Major Wars,* ed. Robert Rotberg and Theodore Rabb (Cambridge: Cambridge University Press, 1989), p. 87. Levy refers to several historical studies that have confirmed the findings of Small and Singer in the *Jerusalem Journal of International Relations,* vol. I, 1976.

65. See Michael Doyle's fine treatise, *Ways of War and Peace* (New York: Norton, 1997), pp. 277–284. The whole of chapter 9 on Kant is relevant. Aspects of Doyle's view appeared earlier in a two-part article, "Kant, Liberal Legacies, and Foreign Affairs," in *PAPA,* vol. 12, Summer/Fall 1983. A survey of evidence is in the first part, pp. 206–232. Doyle writes on page 213: "These conventions [based on the international implications of liberal principles and institutions] of mutual respect have formed

None of the more famous wars of history was between settled liberal democratic peoples. Certainly not the Peloponnesian war, since neither Athens nor Sparta was a liberal democracy;[66] and similarly not the Second Punic war between Rome and Carthage, though Rome had some features of republican institutions. As for the religious wars of the sixteenth and seventeenth centuries, since freedom of religion and liberty of conscience were not recognized, none of those states involved qualify as constitutionally democratic. The great wars of the nineteenth century—the Napoleonic wars, Bismarck's war,[67] and the American Civil War—were not between liberal democratic peoples. Germany under Bismarck never had a properly established constitutional regime; and the American South, with nearly half of its population slaves, was not a democracy, though it may have thought of itself as such. In wars in which a number of major powers were engaged, such as the two World Wars, democratic states have fought as allies on the same side.

The absence of war between major established democracies is as close as anything we know to a simple empirical regularity in relations

---

cooperative foundations for relations among liberal democracies of a remarkably effective kind. Even though liberal states have become involved in numerous wars with nonliberal states, *constitutionally secure liberal states have yet to engage in war with one another.* No one should argue that such wars are impossible; but preliminary evidence does appear to indicate . . . a significant predisposition against warfare between liberal states." See also Bruce Russett, *Grasping the Democratic Peace* (Princeton: Princeton University Press, 1993), and John Oneal and Bruce Russett, "The Classical Liberals Were Right: Democracy, Independence, and Conflict," *International Studies Quarterly,* June 1997. Oneal and Russett hold that three factors reduce the likelihood of conflict among nations: shared democracy, mutual trade and commerce, and membership in international and regional organizations. The relevance of the third element would arise in following the Law of Peoples and is hence fully allowed for. Membership in these organizations presumably establishes diplomatic ties, making it easier to manage potential conflicts.

66. It is enough to say that they both had slaves. Although the cultural glories of Athens are real, one cannot ignore the fact of slavery or that the 30,000 or so who could attend the assembly were autocrats ruling over a population of 300,000, slaves and aliens, artisans and women.

67. By this I mean the three wars he connived to bring about Prussia's conquest of Germany: Schleswig-Holstein (1864), the Austrian-Prussian War (1866), and the Franco-Prussian War (1870–1871).

among societies.[68] From this fact, I should like to think the historical record shows that a society of democratic peoples, all of whose basic institutions are well-ordered by liberal conceptions of right and justice (though not necessarily by the same conception), is stable for the right reasons. As Michael Doyle has noted, however, an enumeration of favorable historical cases is hardly sufficient, since the idea of democratic peace sometimes fails. In these cases, my guiding hypothesis leads me to expect to find various failures in a democracy's essential supporting institutions and practices.

Hence, given the great shortcomings of actual, allegedly constitutional democratic regimes, it is no surprise that they should often intervene in weaker countries, including those exhibiting some aspects of a democracy, or even that they should engage in war for expansionist reasons. As for the first situation, the United States overturned the democracies of Allende in Chile, Arbenz in Guatemala, Mossadegh in Iran, and, some would add, the Sandanistas in Nicaragua. Whatever the merits of these regimes, covert operations against them were carried out by a government prompted by monopolistic and oligarchic interests without the knowledge or criticism of the public. This subterfuge was made easier by the handy appeal to national security in the context of superpower rivalry, which allowed such weak democracies to be cast, however implausibly, as a danger. Though democratic peoples are not expansionist, they do defend their security interest, and a democratic government can easily invoke this interest to support covert interventions, even when actually moved by economic interests behind the scenes.[69]

Of course nations that are now established constitutional democracies have in the past engaged in empire building. A number of European nations did so in the eighteenth and nineteenth centuries and

68. See Levy's "Domestic Politics and War," p. 88. In the studies to which he refers, most definitions of democracy are comparable to that of Small and Singer. Levy lists the elements of their definition in a footnote: (1) regular elections and the participation of opposition parties; (2) the participation of at least 10 percent of the adult population; (3) the institution of a parliament either controlling or sharing parity with an executive branch. Our definition of a liberal democratic regime goes well beyond this definition.

69. On this point see Allan Gilbert, "Power Motivated Democracy," *Political Theory,* November 1992, esp. pp. 684ff.

during the rivalry among Great Britain, France, and Germany before World War I. England and France fought a war for empire—the so-called Seven Years' War—in the mid-eighteenth century. France lost its colonies in North America, and England lost its American colonies after the Revolution of 1776. I cannot offer here an explanation of the events of these centuries, as it would involve examining the class structure of these nations over time, and how that structure affected the desire of England and France for colonies as early as the seventeenth century, as well as the role of the armed forces in supporting this desire. It would also involve a study of the role played in an age of mercantilism by chartered trading companies (awarded a monopoly by the Crown), such as the East India Company and the Hudson Bay Company.[70] Clearly the shortcomings of these societies as constitutional democracies with their required support elements—(a) to (e) above—are evident even from a cursory inquiry. Thus, whether Kant's hypothesis of a *foedus pacificum* is met depends on how far the conditions of a family of constitutional regimes attain the ideal of such regimes with their supporting elements. If the hypothesis is correct, armed conflict between democratic peoples will tend to disappear as they approach that ideal, and they will engage in war only as allies in self-defense against outlaw states. I believe this hypothesis is correct and think it underwrites the Law of Peoples as a realistic utopia.

§6. Society of Liberal Peoples: Its Public Reason

6.1. Society of Peoples and Reasonable Pluralism. What can be the basis for a Society of Peoples given the reasonable and expected differences of peoples from one another, with their distinctive institutions

---

70. On these matters and their economic effects, see Adam Smith's *The Wealth of Nations* (1776) and Joseph Schumpeter's "The Sociology of Imperialisms," in *Imperialism and Social Classes* (1917), ed. Paul Sweezy (New York: Kelley, 1951). See also Albert Hirschman's *Rival Views of Market Society;* note what he says about the feudal-shackles thesis, pp. 126–132. Relevant also is Michael Doyle, *The Ways of War and Peace,* chapter 7, where he discusses the idea of commercial pacifism, which goes back to the eighteenth century, and of which Smith and Schumpeter are important representatives.

and languages, religions and cultures, as well as their different histories, variously situated as they are in different regions and territories of the world and experiencing different events? (These differences parallel the fact of reasonable pluralism in a domestic regime.)

To see how to obtain a basis, I repeat what I said in the Introduction: it is important to understand that the Law of Peoples is developed within political liberalism. This beginning point means that the Law of Peoples is an extension of a liberal conception of justice for a *domestic* regime to a *Society of Peoples.* Developing the Law of Peoples within a liberal conception of justice, we work out the ideals and principles of the foreign policy of a reasonably just liberal people. I distinguish between the public reason of liberal peoples and the public reason of the Society of Peoples. The first is the public reason of equal citizens of domestic society debating the constitutional essentials and matters of basic justice concerning their own government; the second is the public reason of free and equal liberal peoples debating their mutual relations as peoples. The Law of Peoples with its political concepts and principles, ideals and criteria, is the content of this latter public reason. Although these two public reasons do not have the same content, the role of public reason among free and equal peoples is analogous to its role in a constitutional democratic regime among free and equal citizens.

Political liberalism proposes that, in a constitutional democratic regime, comprehensive doctrines of truth or of right are to be replaced in public reason by an idea of the politically reasonable addressed to citizens as citizens. Here note the parallel: public reason is invoked by members of the Society of Peoples, and its principles are addressed to peoples as peoples. They are not expressed in terms of comprehensive doctrines of truth or of right, which may hold sway in this or that society, but in terms that can be shared by different peoples.

6.2. Ideal of Public Reason. Distinct from the idea of public reason is the *ideal* of public reason. In domestic society this ideal is realized, or satisfied, whenever judges, legislators, chief executives, and other government officials, as well as candidates for public office, act from and follow the idea of public reason and explain to other citizens their reasons for supporting fundamental political questions in terms of the political conception of justice that they regard as the most reasonable. In this way they fulfill what I shall call their duty of civility to one another and to other citizens. Hence whether judges, legislators, and chief executives act from and follow public reason is continually shown in their speech and conduct.

How is the ideal of public reason realized by citizens who are not government officials? In a representative government, citizens vote for representatives—chief executives, legislators, and the like—not for particular laws (except at a state or local level where they may vote directly on referenda questions, which are not usually fundamental questions). To answer this question, we say that, ideally, citizens are to think of themselves *as if* they were legislators and ask themselves what statutes, supported by what reasons satisfying the criterion of reciprocity, they would think it most reasonable to enact.[71] When firm and widespread, the disposition of citizens to view themselves as ideal legislators, and to repudiate government officials and candidates for public office who violate public reason, forms part of the political and social basis of liberal democracy and is vital for its enduring strength and vigor. Thus in domestic society citizens fulfill their duty of civility and support the idea of public reason, while doing what they can to hold government officials to it. This duty, like other political rights and duties, is an intrinsically moral duty. I emphasize that it is not a legal duty, for in that case it would be incompatible with freedom of speech.

Similarly, the ideal of the public reason of free and equal peoples is realized, or satisfied, whenever chief executives and legislators, and other government officials, as well as candidates for public office, act from and follow the principles of the Law of Peoples and explain to other peoples their reasons for pursuing or revising a people's foreign policy and affairs of state that involve other societies. As for private citizens, we say, as before, that ideally citizens are to think of themselves *as if* they were executives and legislators and ask themselves what foreign policy supported by what considerations they would think it most rea-

71. There is some resemblance between this criterion and Kant's principle of the original contract. See *Metaphysics of Morals, Doctrine of Right*, §§47–49, and "Theory and Practice," part II.

sonable to advance. Once again, when firm and widespread, the disposition of citizens to view themselves as ideal executives and legislators, and to repudiate government officials and candidates for public office who violate the public reason of free and equal peoples, is part of the political and social basis of peace and understanding among peoples.

6.3. Content of the Law of Peoples. Recall that, in the domestic case,[72] the content of public reason is given by the family of liberal principles of justice for a constitutional democratic regime, and not by a single one. There are many liberalisms and therefore many forms of public reason specified by the family of reasonable political conceptions. Our task in developing the public reason of the Society of Peoples was to specify its content—its ideals, principles, and standards—and how they apply to the political relations among peoples. And this we did in the first argument in the original position at the second level when I considered the merits of the eight principles of the Law of Peoples listed in §4. These familiar and largely traditional principles I took from the history and usages of international law and practice. As I said in §4, the parties are not given a menu of alternative principles and ideals from which to select, as they were in *Political Liberalism,* and in *A Theory of Justice.* Rather, the representatives of liberal constitutional democracies reflect on the advantages of the principles of equality among peoples. The principles must also satisfy the criterion of reciprocity, since this criterion holds at both levels—both between citizens as citizens and between peoples as peoples. In the latter case it requires that, in proposing a principle to regulate the mutual relations between peoples, a people or their representatives must think not only that it is reasonable for them to propose it, but also that it is reasonable for other peoples to accept it.

6.4. Conclusion. We have just completed in §§3–5 the first step of ideal theory. When can we reasonably accept this first step of the Law of Peoples as provisionally sound and justified?

(i) We must find the reasoning in the second original position for

---

72. See "The Idea of Public Reason Revisited."

principles and standards of the Law of Peoples highly plausible and capable of further support. The account of stability for the right reasons must strike us as equally convincing.

(ii) The view of democratic peace should also be plausible and well-supported by the historical record of the conduct of democratic peoples. It must also be confirmed by the guiding hypothesis that democracies fully satisfying the essential supporting conditions, (a) through (e), remain at peace with one another.

(iii) Finally, we must be able, as citizens of liberal societies, to endorse, on due reflection, the principles and judgments of the Law of Peoples. The social contract conception of that law, more than any other conception known to us, should tie together, into one coherent view, our considered political convictions and political (moral) judgments at all levels of generality.

In the next part, I discuss decent hierarchical peoples in §§8–9. In Part III I discuss the two steps of *nonideal* theory. The reason for going on to consider the point of view of decent hierarchical peoples is not to prescribe principles of justice for *them,* but to assure ourselves that liberal principles of foreign policy are also reasonable from a decent nonliberal point of view. The desire to achieve this assurance is intrinsic to the liberal conception.

The Second Part of Ideal Theory

§7. Toleration of Nonliberal Peoples

7.1. Meaning of Toleration. A main task in extending the Law of Peoples to nonliberal peoples is to specify how far liberal peoples are to tolerate nonliberal peoples. Here, to tolerate means not only to refrain from exercising political sanctions—military, economic, or diplomatic—to make a people change its ways. To tolerate also means to recognize these nonliberal societies as equal participating members in good standing of the Society of Peoples, with certain rights and obligations, including the duty of civility requiring that they offer other peoples public reasons appropriate to the Society of Peoples for their actions.

Liberal societies are to cooperate with and assist all peoples in good standing. If all societies were required to be liberal, then the idea of political liberalism would fail to express due toleration for other acceptable ways (if such there are, as I assume) of ordering society. We recognize that a liberal society is to respect its citizens' comprehensive doctrines—religious, philosophical, and moral—provided that these doctrines are pursued in ways compatible with a reasonable political conception of justice and its public reason. Similarly, we say that, provided a nonliberal society's basic institutions meet certain specified conditions of political right and justice and lead its people to honor a reasonable and just law for the Society of Peoples, a liberal people is to tolerate and accept that society. In the absence of a better name, I call societies that satisfy these conditions *decent* peoples (§8.2).

7.2. Need for Conception of Toleration. Some may say that there is no need for the Law of Peoples to develop such an idea of toleration. The reason they might give is that citizens in a liberal society should judge other societies by how closely their ideals and institutions express and realize a reasonable liberal political conception. Given the fact of pluralism, citizens in a liberal society affirm a family of reasonable political conceptions of justice and will differ as to which conception is the most reasonable. But they agree that nonliberal societies fail to treat persons who possess all the powers of reason, intellect, and moral feeling as truly free and equal, and *therefore,* they say, nonliberal societies are always properly subject to some form of sanction—political, economic, or even military—depending on the case. On this view, the guiding principle of liberal foreign policy is gradually to shape all not yet liberal societies in a liberal direction, until eventually (in the ideal case) all societies are liberal.

The italicized "therefore" several lines back marks, however, an inference that begs the following question: how do we know, before trying to work out a reasonable Law of Peoples, that nonliberal societies are always, other things being equal, the proper object of political sanctions? As we have seen in discussing the arguments in the second original position in which the principles of the Law of Peoples are selected for liberal peoples, the parties are the representatives of equal peoples, and equal peoples will want to maintain this equality with each other. Morover, what the representatives of peoples select among are interpretations of the eight principles listed in §4. No people will be willing to count the losses to itself as outweighed by gains to other peoples; and therefore the principle of utility, and other moral principles discussed in moral philosophy, are not even candidates for a Law of Peoples. As I explain later, this consequence, which is implied by the very procedure of extending the liberal conception of political justice from the domestic case to the Law of Peoples, will also hold for the further extension to decent peoples.

7.3. Basic Structure of Society of Peoples. A further important consideration is the following: if liberal peoples require that all societies be liberal and subject those that are not to politically enforced sanctions, then decent nonliberal peoples—if there are such—will be denied a due measure of respect by liberal peoples. This lack of respect may wound the self-respect of decent nonliberal peoples as peoples, as well as their individual members, and may lead to great bitterness and resentment. Denying respect to other peoples and their members requires strong reasons to be justified. Liberal peoples cannot say that decent peoples deny human rights, since (as we shall see in §§8–9 where the notion of decency is developed) such peoples recognize and protect these rights; nor can liberal peoples say that decent peoples deny their members the right to be consulted or a substantial political role in making decisions, since the basic structure of these societies will be seen to include a *decent consultation hierarchy* or its equivalent. Finally, decent peoples allow a right of dissent, and government and judicial officials are required to give a respectful reply, one that addresses the merits of the question according to the rule of law as interpreted by the judiciary. Dissenters may not be dismissed as simply incompetent or lacking in understanding. In this and other ways, the common good conception of justice held by decent peoples may gradually change over time, prodded by the dissents of members of these peoples.

All societies undergo gradual changes, and this is no less true of decent societies than of others. Liberal peoples should not suppose that decent societies are unable to reform themselves in their own way. By recognizing these societies as *bona fide* members of the Society of Peoples, liberal peoples encourage this change. They do not in any case stifle such change, as withholding respect from decent peoples might well do. Leaving aside the deep question of whether some forms of culture and ways of life are good in themselves (as I believe they are), it is surely, *ceteris paribus,* a good for individuals and associations to be attached to their particular culture and to take part in its common public and civic life. In this way political society is expressed and fulfilled.

This is no small thing. It argues for preserving significant room for the idea of a people's self-determination and for some kind of loose or confederate form of a Society of Peoples. Recall that peoples (as op-

posed to states) have a definite moral nature (§2.1). This nature includes
a certain proper pride and sense of honor; peoples may take a proper
pride in their histories and achievements, as what I call a "proper patriotism" allows (§5.1). The due respect they ask for is a due respect consistent with the equality of all peoples. The interests that move peoples
(and distinguish them from states) are congruent with a fair equality
and a due respect for other peoples. Liberal peoples must try to encourage decent peoples and not frustrate their vitality by coercively insisting
that all societies be liberal. Moreover, if a liberal constitutional democracy is, in fact, superior to other forms of society, as I believe it to be, a
liberal people should have confidence in their convictions and suppose
that a decent society, when offered due respect by liberal peoples, may be
more likely, over time, to recognize the advantages of liberal institutions
and take steps toward becoming more liberal on its own.

In the last three paragraphs I have tried to suggest the great importance of all decent peoples' maintaining their self-respect and having
the respect of other liberal or decent peoples. Certainly the social
world of liberal and decent peoples is not one that, by liberal principles, is fully just. Some may feel that permitting this injustice and not
insisting on liberal principles for all societies requires strong reasons. I
believe that there are such reasons. Most important is maintaining mutual respect among peoples. Lapsing into contempt on the one side,
and bitterness and resentment on the other, can only cause damage.
These relations are not a matter of the internal (liberal or decent) basic
structure of each people viewed separately. Rather, maintaining mutual respect among peoples in the Society of Peoples constitutes an essential part of the basic structure and political climate of that society.
The Law of Peoples considers this wider background basic structure
and the merits of its political climate in encouraging reforms in a liberal direction as overriding the lack of liberal justice in decent societies.

§8. Extension to Decent Hierarchical Peoples

8.1. Procedural Remarks. Recall that, in ideal theory, the extension
of liberal political ideas of right and justice to the Law of Peoples pro-

ceeds in two steps. The first step we completed in §§3–5: namely, the extension of the Law of Peoples to liberal societies only. The second step of ideal theory is more difficult: it challenges us to specify a second kind of society—a decent, though not a liberal society—to be recognized as a *bona fide* member of a politically reasonable Society of Peoples and in this sense "tolerated." We must try to formulate the criteria for a decent society. Our aim is to extend the Law of Peoples to decent societies and to show that they accept the same Law of Peoples that liberal societies do. This shared law describes the kind of Society of Peoples that all liberal and decent societies want, and it expresses the regulative end of their foreign policies.

In the Introduction I wrote that, in the political and social world I consider, there are five types of domestic societies: the first of these is *liberal peoples,* and the second, *decent peoples.* The basic structure of one kind of decent people has what I call a "decent consultation hierarchy," and these peoples I call "decent hierarchical peoples"; the other kind of decent people is simply a category I leave in reserve, supposing that there may be other decent peoples whose basic structure does not fit my description of a consultation hierarchy, but who are worthy of membership in a Society of Peoples. I do not try to describe these possible societies. (Liberal peoples and decent peoples I refer to together as "well-ordered peoples.") In addition, there are, third, *outlaw states* and, fourth, *societies burdened by unfavorable conditions.* Finally, fifth, we have societies that are *benevolent absolutisms:* they honor most human rights, but because they deny their members a meaningful role in making political decisions, they are not well-ordered.

In this section I first state two criteria for any decent hierarchical regime. Although these criteria would also be satisfied by a liberal democratic regime, it will become clear as we proceed that they do not require that a society be liberal. Next, we confirm that, in an appropriate original position (at the second level) with a veil of ignorance, the parties representing these decent hierarchical peoples are fairly situated, rational, and moved by appropriate reasons. Once again, the original position functions here as a model of representation, only in this case for working out a Law of Peoples among decent hierarchical peoples. Finally, given their fundamental interests as specified by the two criteria, the parties representing decent hierarchical societies adopt the same Law of Peoples that the parties representing liberal societies adopt. (As I have said, I shall not discuss other possible kinds of decent peoples.)

In §9.3 I give an example of an imaginary decent hierarchical Muslim people whom I have named "Kazanistan." Kazanistan honors and respects human rights, and its basic structure contains a decent consultation hierarchy, thereby giving a substantial political role to its members in making political decisions.

8.2. Two Criteria for Decent Hierarchical Societies. These societies may assume many institutional forms, religious and secular. All these societies, however, are what I call *associationist* in form: that is, the members of these societies are viewed in public life as members of different groups, and each group is represented in the legal system by a body in a decent consultation hierarchy. The two criteria discussed below specify the conditions for a decent hierarchical society to be a member in good standing in a reasonable Society of Peoples. (Many religious and philosophical doctrines with their different ideas of justice may lead to institutions satisfying these conditions. Yet, because these ideas of justice are part of a comprehensive religious or philosophical doctrine, they do not specify a political conception of justice in my sense.)

1. First, the society does not have aggressive aims, and it recognizes that it must gain its legitimate ends through diplomacy and trade and other ways of peace. Although its religious or other underlying doctrine is assumed to be comprehensive and to have influence on the structure of government and its social policy, the society respects the political and social order of other societies. If it does seek wider influence, it does so in ways compatible with the independence of other societies, including their religious and civil liberties. This feature of the society's comprehensive doctrine supports the institutional basis of its peaceful conduct and distinguishes it from the leading European states during the religious wars of the sixteenth and seventeenth centuries.

2. The second criterion has three parts.

(a) The first part is that a decent hierarchical people's system of law, in accordance with its common good idea of justice (see §9), secures for all members of the people what have come to be called human rights. A social system that violates these rights cannot specify a decent scheme of political and social cooperation. A slave society lacks a decent system of law, as its slave economy is driven by a scheme of commands imposed by force. It lacks the idea of social cooperation. (In §9 below I discuss the common good idea of justice in more detail in connection with the idea of a decent consultation hierarchy.)

Among the human rights are the right to life (to the means of subsistence and security);[1] to liberty (to freedom from slavery, serfdom, and forced occupation, and to a sufficient measure of liberty of conscience to ensure freedom of religion and thought);[2] to property (personal property); and to formal equality as expressed by the rules of natural justice (that is, that similar cases be treated similarly).[3] Human rights, as thus understood, cannot be rejected as peculiarly liberal or special to the Western tradition. They are not politically parochial.[4] These matters will be taken up again in §10.

(b) The second part is that a decent people's system of law must be such as to impose *bona fide* moral duties and obligations

1. See Henry Shue, *Basic Rights: Substance, Affluence, and U.S. Foreign Policy* (Princeton: Princeton University Press, 1980). Shue, p. 23, and R. J. Vincent, in his *Human Rights and International Relations,* interpret subsistence as including minimum economic security, and both hold subsistence rights as basic. I agree, since the sensible and rational exercise of all liberties, of whatever kind, as well as the intelligent use of property, always implies having general all-purpose economic means.

2. As discussed in §9.2, this liberty of conscience may not be as extensive nor as equal for all members of society: for instance, one religion may legally predominate in the state government, while other religions, though tolerated, may be denied the right to hold certain positions. I refer to this kind of situation as permitting "liberty of conscience, though not an equal liberty."

3. On the rules of natural justice, see Hart, *The Concept of Law,* pp. 156ff.

4. T. M. Scanlon emphasizes this point in "Human Rights as a Neutral Concern," in *Human Rights and U.S. Foreign Policy,* ed. P. Brown and D. MacLean (Lexington, Mass.: Lexington Books, 1979), pp. 83, 89–92. It is relevant when we note that the support for human rights should be part of the foreign policy of well-ordered societies.

(distinct from human rights) on all persons within the people's territory.[5] Since the members of the people are viewed as decent and rational, as well as responsible and able to play a part in social life, they recognize these duties and obligations as fitting with their common good idea of justice and do not see their duties and obligations as mere commands imposed by force. They have the capacity for moral learning and know the difference between right and wrong as understood in their society. In contrast to a slave economy, their system of law specifies a decent scheme of political and social cooperation.

A decent hierarchical society's conception of the person, as implied by the second criterion, does not require acceptance of the liberal idea that persons are citizens first and have equal basic rights as equal citizens. Rather it views persons as responsible and cooperating members of their respective groups. Hence, persons can recognize, understand, and act in accordance with their moral duties and obligations as members of these groups.

(c) Finally, the third part of the second criterion is that there must be a sincere and not unreasonable belief on the part of judges and other officials who administer the legal system that the law is indeed guided by a common good idea of justice. Laws supported merely by force are grounds for rebellion and resistance. It would be unreasonable, if not irrational, for judges and other officials to think that the common good idea of justice, which assigns human rights to all members of a people, is being

5. Here I draw upon Philip Soper's *A Theory of Law* (Cambridge, Mass.: Harvard University Press, 1984), especially pp. 125–147. Soper holds that a system of law, as distinct from a system of mere commands coercively enforced, must be such as to give rise to moral duties and obligations for all members of society. For a system of law to be maintained, judges and other officials must sincerely and reasonably believe that the law is guided by a common good idea of justice. I don't, however, follow Soper in all respects. A scheme of rules must satisfy his definition to qualify as a proper system of law; see chapter IV, pp. 91–100. But I want to avoid the long-debated jurisprudential problem of the definition of law, and I also don't want to argue that the antebellum South, say, didn't have a system of law. So I see the second part of the above criterion— that a decent people's system of law must be such as to impose *bona fide* moral duties and obligations—as following from a liberal conception of justice extended to the Law of Peoples. I am indebted to Samuel Freeman for valuable discussion of these points.

followed when those rights are systematically violated. This sincere and reasonable belief on the part of judges and officials must be shown in their good faith and willingness to defend publicly society's injunctions as justified by law. The courts serve as a forum for this defense.[6]

8.3. Basis of the Two Criteria. Just as with the idea of the reasonable in political liberalism, there is no definition of decency from which the two criteria can be deduced (see §12.2). Instead we say that the two criteria seem acceptable in their general statement.[7] I think of decency as a normative idea of the same kind as reasonableness, though weaker (that is, it covers less than reasonableness does). We give it meaning by how we use it. Thus, a decent people must honor the laws of peace; its system of law must be such as to respect human rights and to impose duties and obligations on all persons in its territory. Its system of law must follow a common good idea of justice that takes into account what it sees as the fundamental interests of everyone in society. And, finally, there must be a sincere and not unreasonable belief on the part of judges and other officials that the law is indeed guided by a common good idea of justice.

This account of decency, like that of reasonableness, is developed by setting out various criteria and explaining their meaning. The reader has to judge whether a decent people, as given by the two criteria, is to be tolerated and accepted as a member in good standing of the Society of Peoples. It is my conjecture that most reasonable citizens of a liberal society will find peoples who meet these two criteria acceptable as peoples in good standing. Not all reasonable persons will, certainly, yet most will.

The two ideas of justice we have discussed stand at opposite poles. The liberal conception is the one from which we start in our own society and regard as sound on due reflection. The decent common good idea of hierarchical peoples is a minimal idea. Its being realized by a

6. Here I adapt Soper's idea, in *A Theory of Law,* pp. 118, 112.
7. A decent consultation hierarchy is discussed in §9.

society renders its institutions worthy of toleration. There may be a wide range of institutional forms satisfying decent hierarchical ideas, but I shall not try to survey them. My aim has been to outline an idea of justice that, though distant from liberal conceptions, still has features that give to societies so regulated the decent moral status required for them to be members in good standing of a reasonable Society of Peoples.

The features of human rights as I have so far described them have been accounted for in two ways. One is to view them as belonging to a reasonably just liberal political conception of justice and as a proper subset of the rights and liberties secured to all free and equal citizens in a constitutional liberal democratic regime. The other is to view them as belonging to an associationist social form (as I have called it) which sees persons first as members of groups—associations, corporations, and estates. As such members, persons have rights and liberties enabling them to meet their duties and obligations and to engage in a decent system of social cooperation. What have come to be called human rights are recognized as necessary conditions of any system of social cooperation. When they are regularly violated, we have command by force, a slave system, and no cooperation of any kind.

These rights do not depend on any particular comprehensive religious doctrine or philosophical doctrine of human nature. The Law of Peoples does not say, for example, that human beings are moral persons and have equal worth in the eyes of God; or that they have certain moral and intellectual powers that entitle them to these rights. To argue in these ways would involve religious or philosophical doctrines that many decent hierarchical peoples might reject as liberal or democratic, or as in some way distinctive of Western political tradition and prejudicial to other cultures. Still, the Law of Peoples does not deny these doctrines.

It is important to see that an agreement on a Law of Peoples ensuring human rights is not an agreement limited only to liberal societies. I shall now try to confirm this point.

8.4. Original Position for Decent Hierarchical Peoples. Decent hierarchical peoples are well-ordered in terms of their own ideas of justice, which satisfy the two criteria. This being so, I submit that their representatives in an appropriate original position would adopt the same eight principles (§4.1) as those I argued would be adopted by the representatives of liberal societies. The argument for this is as follows: decent hierarchical peoples do not engage in aggressive war; therefore their representatives respect the civic order and integrity of other peoples and accept the symmetrical situation (the equality) of the original position as fair. Next, in view of the common good ideas of justice held in decent hierarchical societies, the representatives strive both to protect the human rights and the good of the people they represent and to maintain their security and independence. The representatives care about the benefits of trade and also accept the idea of assistance among peoples in time of need. Hence, we can say that the representatives of hierarchical societies are decent and rational. In view of this reasoning, we can also say that the members of decent hierarchical societies would accept—as you and I would accept[8]—the original position as fair among peoples, and would endorse the Law of Peoples adopted by their representatives as specifying fair terms of political cooperation with other peoples.

As I noted earlier in discussing the need for an idea of toleration (§7.2–3), some may object that treating the representatives of peoples equally when equality does not hold within their domestic societies is inconsistent, or unfair. The intuitive force of equality holds, it might be said, only between individuals, and treating societies equally depends on their treating their members equally. I don't agree. Instead, equality holds between reasonable or decent, and rational, individuals or collectives of various kinds when the relation of equality between them is appropriate for the case at hand. An example: in certain matters, churches may be treated equally and are to be consulted as equals on policy questions—the Catholic and the Congregational churches, for instance. This can be sound practice, it seems, even though the first is hierarchically organized, while the second is not. A second example: universities also may be organized in many ways. Some may choose their presidents by a kind of consultation hierarchy including all rec-

---

8. Here you and I are members of decent hierarchical societies, but not the same one.

ognized groups, others by elections in which all their members, including undergraduates, have a vote. In some cases the members have only one vote; other arrangements allow plural voting depending on the voter's status. But the fact that universities' internal arrangements differ doesn't rule out the propriety of treating them as equals in certain circumstances. Further examples can easily be imagined.[9]

Clearly, I have supposed that the representatives of peoples are to be situated equally, even though the ideas of justice of the decent nonliberal societies they represent allow basic inequalities among their members. (For example, some members may not be granted what I call "equal liberty of conscience"; see note 2 above.) There is, however, no inconsistency: a people sincerely affirming a nonliberal idea of justice may still reasonably think its society should be treated equally in a reasonably just Law of Peoples. Although full equality may be lacking within a society, equality may be reasonably put forward in making claims against other societies.

Note that, in the case of a decent hierarchical society, there is no original position argument deriving the form of its basic structure. As it is used in a social contract conception, an original position argument for domestic justice is a liberal idea, and it does not apply to the domestic justice of a decent hierarchical regime. That is why the Law of Peoples uses an original position argument only three times: twice for liberal societies (once at the domestic level and once at the Law of Peoples level), but only once, at the second level, for decent hierarchical societies. Only equal parties can be symmetrically situated in an original position. Equal peoples, or their representatives, are equal parties at the level of the Law of Peoples. At another level, it makes sense to think of liberal and decent peoples together in an original position when joining together into regional associations or federations of some kind, such as the European Community, or the commonwealth of the republics in the former Soviet Union. It is natural to envisage future world society as in good part composed of such federations together with certain institutions, such as the United Nations, capable of speaking for all the societies of the world.

9. I am indebted to Thomas Nagel for discussion of this question.

§9. Decent Consultation Hierarchy

9.1. Consultation Hierarchy and Common Aim. The first two parts of the second criterion require that a decent hierarchical society's system of law be guided by what I have called a common good idea of justice.[10] But the meaning of such an idea is not yet clear. I try to spell it out further, first, by distinguishing it from the common aim of a people (if they have one) and, second, by insisting that the legal system of a decent hierarchical people must contain a decent consultation hierarchy. That is, the basic structure of the society must include a family of representative bodies whose role in the hierarchy is to take part in an established procedure of consultation and to look after what the people's common good idea of justice regards as the important interests of all members of the people.

The common aim or end (should there be one) is what the society as a whole tries to achieve for itself or its members. The common aim or end affects what persons receive and their well-being. In the common good idea of justice the pursuit of this common aim is to be encouraged, but is not to be maximized in and of itself, but rather maximized consistent with the restrictions specified by honoring the steps in the consultation procedure, which provides the institutional basis for protecting the rights and duties of the members of the people. (Many societies do not have a common aim but rather what I shall call "special priorities" [§9.3]. In this case also, these priorities must be pursued in a manner consistent with the restrictions specified by the consultation procedure.)

Although all persons in a decent hierarchical society are not regarded as free and equal citizens, nor as separate individuals deserving equal representation (according to the maxim: one citizen, one vote), they are seen as decent and rational and as capable of moral learning as recognized in their society. As responsible members of society, they can recognize when their moral duties and obligations accord with the people's common good idea of justice. Each person belongs to a group

10. Well-ordered societies with liberal conceptions of political justice also have a common good conception in this sense: namely, the common good of achieving political justice for all its citizens over time and preserving the free culture that justice allows.

represented by a body in the consultation hierarchy, and each person engages in distinctive activities and plays a certain role in the overall scheme of cooperation.

In political decisions a decent consultation hierarchy allows an opportunity for different voices to be heard—not, to be sure, in a way allowed by democratic institutions, but appropriately in view of the religious and philosophical values of the society as expressed in its idea of the common good. Persons as members of associations, corporations, and estates have the right at some point in the procedure of consultation (often at the stage of selecting a group's representatives) to express political dissent, and the government has an obligation to take a group's dissent seriously and to give a conscientious reply. It is necessary and important that different voices be heard, because judges' and other officials' sincere belief in the justice of the legal system must include respect for the possibility of dissent.[11] Judges and other officials must be willing to address objections. They cannot refuse to listen, charging that the dissenters are incompetent and unable to understand, for then we would have not a decent consultation hierarchy, but a paternalistic regime.[12] Moreover, should the judges and other officials listen, the dissenters are not required to accept the answer given to them; they may renew their protest, provided they explain why they are still dissatisfied, and their explanation in turn ought to receive a further and fuller reply. Dissent expresses a form of public protest and is permissible provided it stays within the basic framework of the common good idea of justice.

9.2. Three Observations. Many points need to be examined before the idea of a decent consultation hierarchy is sufficiently clear. I note three.

A first observation concerns why there are groups represented by bodies in the consultation hierarchy. (In the liberal scheme, separate citizens are so represented.) One answer is that a decent hierarchical society might hold a view similar to Hegel's, which goes as follows: in

---

11. See Soper, *A Theory of Law,* p. 141.

12. The procedure of consultation is often mentioned in discussions of Islamic political institutions; yet it is clear that the purpose of consultation is often so that the Caliph can obtain a commitment of loyalty from his subjects, or sometimes so that he can discern the strength of the opposition.

the well-ordered decent society, persons belong first to estates, corporations, and associations—that is, groups. Since these groups represent
the rational interests of their members, some persons will take part in
publicly representing these interests in the consultation process, but
they do so as members of associations, corporations, and estates, and
not as individuals. The justification for this arrangement is as follows:
whereas, so the view goes, in a liberal society, where each citizen has
one vote, citizens' interests tend to shrink and center on their private
economic concerns to the detriment of the bonds of community, in a
consultation hierarchy, when their group is so represented, the voting
members of the various groups take into account the broader interests
of political life. Of course, a decent hierarchical society has never had
the concept of one person, one vote, which is associated with a liberal
democratic tradition of thought that is foreign to it, and perhaps
would think (as Hegel did) that such an idea mistakenly expresses an
individualistic idea that each person, as an atomistic unit, has the basic
right to participate equally in political deliberation.[13]

13. See Hegel, *Philosophy of Right* (1821), §308. Hegel's main objection to the Constitution of Würtemberg presented by the liberal King in 1815–1816 fixes on its idea of
direct suffrage. His objection is found in part in the following passage from the essay of
1817, "The Proceedings of the Estates Assembly in the Kingdom of Würtemberg, 1815–
1816": "The electors appear otherwise in no bond or connexion with the civil order and
the organization of the state. The citizens come to the scene as isolated atoms, and the
electoral assemblies as unordered inorganic aggregates; the people as a whole are dis-
solved into a heap. This is a form in which the community should never have appeared at
all in undertaking any enterprise; it is a form most unworthy of the community and most
in contradiction with its concepts as a spiritual order. Age and property are qualities
affecting only the individual himself, not characteristically constituting his worth in the
civil order. Such worth he has only on the strength of his office, his position, his skill in
craftsmanship which, recognized by his fellow citizens, entitles him accordingly to be described as master of his craft" (p. 262). The passage continues along these lines and concludes by saying: "On the other hand, of one who is only twenty-five years old and the
owner of real estate that brings him 200 or more guilders a year, we say 'he is nothing.' If
the constitution nevertheless makes him something, a voter, it grants him lofty political
right without any tie with other civic bodies and introduces one of the most important
matters in a situation which has more in common with the democratic, even anarchical,
principle of separation than with that of an organic order" (pp. 262–263). Despite these
objections, Hegel took the side of the liberal constitution of the King against the conser-
vative estates. I cite the translation of Hegel's essay in *Hegel's Political Writings*, trans.
T. M. Knox with an introduction by Z. A. Pelczynski (Oxford: Clarendon Press, 1964).

Second, the nature of a decent people's view of religious toleration needs explicit mention. Although in decent hierarchical societies a state religion may, on some questions, be the ultimate authority within society and may control government policy on certain important matters, that authority is not (as I have already stressed) extended politically to relations with other societies. Further, a decent hierarchical society's (comprehensive) religious or philosophical doctrines must not be fully unreasonable. By this I mean, among other things, that these doctrines must admit a sufficient measure of liberty of conscience and freedom of religion and thought, even if these freedoms are not as extensive nor as equal for all members of the decent society as they are in liberal societies. Although the established religion may have various privileges, it is essential to the society's being decent that no religion be persecuted, or denied civic and social conditions permitting its practice in peace and without fear.[14] Moreover, in view of the possible inequality of religious freedom, if for no other reason, it is essential that a hierarchical society allow and provide assistance for the right of emigration.[15]

The question might arise here as to why religious or philosophical doctrines that deny full and equal liberty of conscience are not unreasonable. I do not say that they are reasonable, but rather that they are not fully unreasonable; one should allow, I think, a space between the fully unreasonable and the fully reasonable. The latter requires full and equal liberty of conscience, and the former denies it entirely. Traditional doctrines that allow a measure of liberty of conscience but do

14. On the importance of this stipulation, see Judith Shklar's *Ordinary Vices* (Cambridge, Mass.: Harvard University Press, 1984), in which she presents what she calls the "liberalism of fear." See especially the introduction and chapters 1 and 6. Shklar once called this kind of liberalism that of "permanent minorities"; see her *Legalism* (Cambridge, Mass.: Harvard University Press, 1964), p. 224.

15. Subject to certain qualifications, liberal societies must also allow for this right. It may be objected that the right of emigration lacks a point without the right to be accepted somewhere as an immigrant. But many rights are without point in this sense: to give a few examples, the right to marry, to invite people into one's house, or even to make a promise. It takes two to make good on these rights. Another complex question is how far the right to emigration should extend. Whatever the answer, certainly the right to emigration for religious minorities should not be merely formal, and a people should provide assistance for emigrants when feasible.

not allow it fully are views that I believe lie in that space and are not fully unreasonable.

A third observation concerns the representation in a consultation hierarchy of members of society, such as women, who may have long been subjected to oppression and abuse, amounting to the violation of their human rights. One step to ensure that their claims are appropriately taken into account may be to arrange that a majority of the members of the bodies representing the (previously) oppressed be chosen from among those whose rights have been violated. As we have seen, one condition of a decent hierarchical society is that its legal system and social order do not violate human rights. The procedure of consultation must be arranged to stop all such violations.[16]

9.3. Kazanistan: A Decent Hierarchical People. The Law of Peoples does not presuppose the existence of actual decent hierarchical peoples any more than it presupposes the existence of actual reasonably just constitutional democratic peoples. If we set the standards very high, neither exists. In the case of democratic peoples, the most we can say is that some are closer than others to a reasonably just constitutional regime. The case of decent hierarchical peoples is even less clear. Can we coherently describe its basic social institutions and political virtues?

Guided by §§8–9, I now describe a hypothetical decent hierarchical people. The purpose of this example is to suggest that a decent government is viable provided that its rulers do not allow themselves to be corrupted, either by favoring the rich or by enjoying the exercise of power for itself. Imagine an idealized Islamic people named "Kazanistan." Kazanistan's system of law does not institute the separation of church and state. Islam is the favored religion, and only Muslims can hold the upper positions of political authority and influence the government's main decisions and policies, including foreign affairs. Yet

---

16. I return to this point in §10. It should be noted here that some writers maintain that full democratic and liberal rights are necessary to prevent violations of human rights. This is stated as an empirical fact supported by historical experience. I do not argue against this contention, and indeed it may be true. But my remarks about a decent hierarchical society are conceptual. I ask, that is, whether we can imagine such a society; and, should it exist, whether we would judge that it should be tolerated politically.

other religions are tolerated and may be practiced without fear or loss of most civic rights, except the right to hold the higher political or judicial offices. (This exclusion marks a fundamental difference between Kazanistan and a liberal democratic regime, where all offices and positions are, in principle, open to each citizen.) Other religions and associations are encouraged to have a flourishing cultural life of their own and to take part in the civic culture of the wider society.[17]

As I imagine it, this decent people is marked by its enlightened treatment of the various non-Islamic religions and other minorities who have been living in its territory for generations, originating from conquests long ago or from immigration which the people permitted. These minorities have been loyal subjects of society, and they are not subjected to arbitrary discrimination, or treated as inferior by Muslims in public or social relations. To try to strengthen their loyalty, the government allows that non-Muslims may belong to the armed forces and serve in the higher ranks of command. Unlike most Muslim rulers, the rulers of Kazanistan have not sought empire and territory. This is in part a result of its theologians' interpreting *jihad* in a spiritual and moral sense, and not in military terms.[18] The Muslim rulers have long held the view that all members of society naturally want to be loyal members of the country into which they are born; and that, unless they are unfairly treated and discriminated against, they will remain so. Following this idea has proved highly successful. Kazanistan's non-

17. Many paths can lead to toleration; on this see Michael Walzer's *On Toleration* (New Haven: Yale University Press, 1997). The doctrine I have attributed to the rulers of Kazanistan was similar to one found in Islam some centuries ago. (The Ottoman Empire tolerated Jews and Christians; the Ottoman rulers even invited them to come to the capital city of Constantinople.) This doctrine affirms the worthiness of all decent religions and provides the essentials of what realistic utopia requires. According to this doctrine: (a) all religious differences between peoples are divinely willed, and this is so whether the believers belong to the same or different societies; (b) punishment for wrong belief is for God alone; (c) communities of different beliefs are to respect one another; (d) belief in natural religion is inborn in all people. These principles are discussed by Roy Mottahedeh in his "Toward an Islamic Theory of Toleration," in *Islamic Law Reform and Human Rights* (Oslo: Nordic Human Rights Publications, 1993).

18. The spiritual interpretation of *jihad* was once common in Islamic countries; under this interpretation, *jihad* was understood to be an obligation of every individual Muslim. See Bernard Lewis, *The Middle East* (New York: Scribner, 1995), pp. 233ff.

Muslim members and its minorities have remained loyal and supported the government in times of danger.

I think it is also plausible to imagine Kazanistan as organized in a decent consultation hierarchy, which has been changed from time to time to make it more sensitive to the needs of its people and the many different groups represented by legal bodies in the consultation hierarchy. This hierarchy satisfies quite closely the following six guidelines. First, all groups must be consulted. Second, each member of a people must belong to a group. Third, each group must be represented by a body that contains at least some of the group's own members who know and share the fundamental interests of the group. These first three conditions ensure that the fundamental interests of all groups are consulted and taken into account.[19] Fourth, the body that makes the final decision—the rulers of Kazanistan—must weigh the views and claims of each of the bodies consulted, and, if called upon, judges and other officials must explain and justify the rulers' decision. In the spirit of the procedure, consultation with each body may influence the outcome. Fifth, the decision should be made according to a conception of the special priorities of Kazanistan. Among these special priorities is to establish a decent and rational Muslim people respecting the religious minorities within it. Here we may expect non-Muslim minorities to be less wedded to certain of the priorities than Muslims, but we may reasonably conjecture, I believe, that both Muslims and non-Muslims will understand and regard these priorities as significant. Sixth and last—but highly important—these special priorities must fit into an overall scheme of cooperation, and the fair terms according to which the group's cooperation is to be conducted should be explicitly specified.[20] This conception is not precise; yet it serves as a guide for decision-making against the background of actual situations and established expectations.

19. This seems closest to John Finnis's first sense of the common good in his *Natural Law and Natural Rights* (Oxford: Clarendon Press, 1980), pp. 155ff.

20. This conception of the common good is close to Finnis's third sense. See again *Natural Law and Natural Rights*, pp. 155ff. Here I reiterate that a consultation hierarchy does not strive simply to maximize achievement of the common aim. Rather, it tries to maximize this achievement consistent with honoring all the restrictions enshrined in the procedure of consultation itself. This is what distinguishes a just or decent society from others.

Finally, I imagine the basic structure of Kazanistan as including assemblies where the bodies in the consultation hierarchy can meet. Here representatives can raise their objections to government policies, and members of the government can express their replies, which the government is required to do. Dissent is respected in the sense that a reply is due that spells out how the government thinks it can both reasonably interpret its policies in line with its common good idea of justice and impose duties and obligations on all members of society. I further imagine, as an example of how dissent, when allowed and listened to, can instigate change, that in Kazanistan dissent has led to important reforms in the rights and role of women, with the judiciary agreeing that existing norms could not be squared with society's common good idea of justice.

I do not hold that Kazanistan is perfectly just, but it does seem to me that such a society is decent. Moreover, even though it is only imagined, I do not think it is unreasonable that a society like Kazanistan might exist, especially as it is not without precedent in the real world (as note 18 above indicates). Readers might charge me with baseless utopianism, but I disagree. Rather, it seems to me that something like Kazanistan is the best we can realistically—and coherently—hope for. It is an enlightened society in its treatment of religious minorities. I think enlightenment about the limits of liberalism recommends trying to conceive a reasonably just Law of Peoples that liberal and nonliberal peoples could together endorse. The alternative is a fatalistic cynicism which conceives the good of life solely in terms of power.

§10. Human Rights

10.1. Law of Peoples Sufficiently Liberal. It may be objected that the Law of Peoples is not sufficiently liberal. This objection might take two forms. For one, some think of human rights as roughly the same rights that citizens have in a reasonable constitutional democratic regime; this view simply expands the class of human rights to include all the rights that liberal governments guarantee. Human rights in the Law of

Peoples, by contrast, express a special class of urgent rights, such as freedom from slavery and serfdom, liberty (but not equal liberty) of conscience, and security of ethnic groups from mass murder and genocide. The violation of this class of rights is equally condemned by both reasonable liberal peoples and decent hierarchical peoples.

A second claim of those who hold that the Law of Peoples is not sufficiently liberal is that only liberal democratic governments are effective in protecting even those human rights specified by the Law of Peoples. According to critics who take this line, this is a fact confirmed by the history of many different countries around the world. Should the facts of history, supported by the reasoning of political and social thought, show that hierarchical regimes are always, or nearly always, oppressive and deny human rights, the case for liberal democracy is made.[21] The Law of Peoples assumes, however, that decent hierarchical peoples exist, or could exist, and considers why they should be tolerated and accepted by liberal peoples as peoples in good standing.

10.2. Role of Human Rights in the Law of Peoples. Human rights are a class of rights that play a special role in a reasonable Law of Peoples: they restrict the justifying reasons for war and its conduct, and they specify limits to a regime's internal autonomy. In this way they reflect the two basic and historically profound changes in how the powers of sovereignty have been conceived since World War II. First, war is no longer an admissible means of government policy and is justified only in self-defense, or in grave cases of intervention to protect human rights. And second, a government's internal autonomy is now limited.

Human rights are distinct from constitutional rights, or from the rights of liberal democratic citizenship,[22] or from other rights that belong to certain kinds of political institutions, both individualist and

21. The Copenhagen Convention of 1990 defended democratic rights as instrumental in this way.

22. See Judith Shklar's illuminating discussion of the rights of democratic citizenship in her *American Citizenship* (Cambridge, Mass.: Harvard University Press, 1991), with her emphasis on the historical significance of slavery.

associationist. Human rights set a necessary, though not sufficient, standard for the decency of domestic political and social institutions. In doing so they limit admissible domestic law of societies in good standing in a reasonably just Society of Peoples.[23] Hence the special class of human rights has these three roles:

1. Their fulfillment is a necessary condition of the decency of a society's political institutions and of its legal order (§§8–9).
2. Their fulfillment is sufficient to exclude justified and forceful intervention by other peoples, for example, by diplomatic and economic sanctions, or in grave cases by military force.
3. They set a limit to the pluralism among peoples.[24]

10.3. Human Rights in Outlaw States. The list of human rights honored by both liberal and decent hierarchical regimes should be understood as universal rights in the following sense: they are intrinsic to the Law of Peoples and have a political (moral) effect whether or not they are supported locally. That is, their political (moral) force extends to all societies, and they are binding on all peoples and societies, includ-

23. This statement can be clarified by distinguishing among the rights that have been listed as human rights in various international declarations. Consider the Universal Declaration of Human Rights of 1948. First, there are human rights proper, illustrated by Article 3: "Everyone has a right to life, liberty and security of person"; and by Article 5: "No one shall be subjected to torture or to cruel, degrading treatment or punishment." Articles 3 to 18 may all be put under this heading of human rights proper, pending certain questions of interpretation. Second, there are human rights that are obvious implications of the first class of rights. The second class of rights covers the extreme cases described by the special conventions on genocide (1948) and on apartheid (1973). These two classes comprise the human rights connected with the common good, as explained in the text above.

Of the other declarations, some seem more aptly described as stating liberal aspirations, such as Article 1 of the Universal Declaration of Human Rights of 1948: "All human beings are born free and equal in dignity and rights. They are endowed with reason and conscience and should act towards one another in a spirit of brotherhood." Others appear to presuppose specific kinds of institutions, such as the right to social security, in Article 22, and the right to equal pay for equal work, in Article 23.

24. See Terry Nardin, *Law, Morality, and the Relations of States* (Princeton: Princeton University Press, 1983), p. 240, citing Luban's "The Romance of the Nation-State," PAPA, vol. 9 (1980): p. 306.

ing outlaw states.[25] An outlaw state that violates these rights is to be condemned and in grave cases may be subjected to forceful sanctions and even to intervention. The propriety of enforcing the Law of Peoples is already clear from our reflections on the two traditional powers of sovereignty (§2.2), and what I shall say later about the duty of assistance will confirm the right to intervention.

It may be asked by what right well-ordered liberal and decent peoples are justified in interfering with an outlaw state on the grounds that this state has violated human rights. Comprehensive doctrines, religious or nonreligious, might base the idea of human rights on a theological, philosophical, or moral conception of the nature of the human person. That path the Law of Peoples does not follow. What I call human rights are, as I have said, a proper subset of the rights possessed by citizens in a liberal constitutional democratic regime, or of the rights of the members of a decent hierarchical society. As we have worked out the Law of Peoples for liberal and decent peoples, these peoples simply do not tolerate outlaw states. This refusal to tolerate those states is a consequence of liberalism and decency. If the political conception of political liberalism is sound, and if the steps we have taken in developing the Law of Peoples are also sound, then liberal and decent peoples have the right, under the Law of Peoples, not to tolerate outlaw states. Liberal and decent peoples have extremely good reasons for their attitude. Outlaw states are aggressive and dangerous; all peoples are safer and more secure if such states change, or are forced to change, their ways. Otherwise, they deeply affect the international climate of power and violence. I return to these matters in Part III on nonideal theory.[26]

25. Peter Jones, "Human Rights: Philosophical or Political," in *National Rights, International Obligations,* ed. Simon Caney, David George, and Peter Jones (Boulder: Westview Press, 1996), interprets my account of human rights in "The Law of Peoples" as published in *On Human Rights: The Oxford Amnesty Lectures* (New York: Basic Books, 1993) in a way that I believe is mistaken. He is correct in seeing that I interpret human rights as a group of rights that both liberal and decent hierarchical peoples would enforce and recognize. It is not clear that he thinks of them as universal and applying to outlaw states.

26. We must at some point face the question of interfering with outlaw states simply for their violation of human rights, even when these states are not dangerous and aggressive, but indeed quite weak. I come back to this serious question in §§14–15, in my discussion of nonideal theory.

§11. Comments on Procedure of the Law of Peoples

11.1. The Place of Cosmopolitan Justice. Having completed the two parts of ideal theory, I pause to make a few comments on the way the Law of Peoples has been set out using a liberal social contract political conception of justice.

Some think that any liberal Law of Peoples, particularly any social contract such law, should begin by first taking up the question of liberal cosmopolitan or global justice for all persons. They argue that in such a view all persons are considered to be reasonable and rational and to possess what I have called "the two moral powers"—a capacity for a sense of justice and a capacity for a conception of the good—which are the basis of political equality both in comprehensive liberalism, as found in Kant or J. S. Mill, and in political liberalism. From this starting point they go on to imagine a global original position with its veil of ignorance behind which all parties are situated symmetrically. Following the kind of reasoning familiar in the original position for the domestic case,[27] the parties would then adopt a first principle that all persons have equal basic rights and liberties. Proceeding this way would straightaway ground human rights in a political (moral) conception of liberal cosmopolitan justice.[28]

To proceed in this way, however, takes us back to where we were in §7.2 (where I considered and rejected the argument that nonliberal societies are always properly subject to some form of sanctions), since it amounts to saying that all persons are to have the equal liberal rights of citizens in a constitutional democracy. On this account, the foreign policy of a liberal people—which it is our concern to elaborate—will be to act gradually to shape all not yet liberal societies in a liberal direction, until eventually (in the ideal case) all societies are liberal. But this foreign policy simply assumes that only a liberal democratic soci-

27. See *A Theory of Justice,* §§4, 24.

28. Brian Barry, in his *Theories of Justice* (Berkeley: University of California Press, 1989), discusses the merits of this procedure. See also Charles Beitz, *Political Theory and International Relations* (Princeton: Princeton University Press, 1979), part III; Thomas Pogge, *Realizing Rawls* (Ithaca, N.Y.: Cornell University Press, 1990), part 3, chaps. 5–6; and David Richards, "International Distributive Justice," *Nomos,* vol. 24 (1982). All seem to have taken this path.

ety can be acceptable. Without trying to work out a reasonable liberal Law of Peoples, we cannot know that nonliberal societies cannot be acceptable. The possibility of a global original position does not show that, and we can't merely assume it.

The Law of Peoples proceeds from the international political world as we see it, and concerns what the foreign policy of a reasonably just liberal people should be. To elaborate this foreign policy, the Law of Peoples discusses two kinds of well-ordered peoples, liberal democratic peoples and decent hierarchical peoples. The law also discusses outlaw states and states suffering from unfavorable conditions. I recognize that my account involves great simplification. Nevertheless, it allows us to examine in a reasonably realistic way what should be the aim of the foreign policy of a liberal democratic people.

11.2. Clarifications about Decent Societies. To repeat, I am not saying that a decent hierarchical society is as reasonable and just as a liberal society. For judged by the principles of a liberal democratic society, a decent hierarchical society clearly does not treat its members equally. A decent society does, however, have a common good political conception of justice (§8.2), and this conception is honored in its decent consultation hierarchy (§9.1). Moreover, it honors a reasonable and just Law of Peoples, the same law that liberal peoples do. That law applies to how peoples treat each other as *peoples.* How peoples treat each other and how they treat their own members are, it is important to recognize, two different things. A decent hierarchical society honors a reasonable and just Law of Peoples even though it does not treat its own members reasonably or justly as free and equal citizens, since it lacks the liberal idea of citizenship.

A decent hierarchical society meets moral and legal requirements sufficient to override the political reasons we might have for imposing sanctions on, or forcibly intervening with, its people and their institutions and culture. It is important to emphasize that the reasons for not imposing sanctions do not boil down solely to the prevention of possible error and miscalculation in dealing with a foreign people. The danger of error, miscalculation, and also arrogance on the part of those who propose sanctions must, of course, be taken into account; yet decent hierarchical societies do have certain institutional features that deserve respect, even if their institutions as a whole are not sufficiently reasonable from the point of view of political liberalism or liberalism generally. Liberal societies may differ widely in many ways: for example, some are far more egalitarian than others.[29] Yet these differences are tolerated in the society of liberal peoples. Might not the institutions of some kinds of hierarchical societies also be similarly tolerable? I believe this to be so.

Thus, I take it as established that, if decent hierarchical societies honor the conditions specified in §§8–9, those societies would be regarded by liberal people, on reflection, as *bona fide* members of a reasonable Society of Peoples. That is what I mean by toleration. Critical objections, based either on political liberalism, or on comprehensive doctrines, both religious and nonreligious, will continue concerning this and all other matters. Raising these objections is the right of liberal peoples and is fully consistent with the liberties and integrity of decent hierarchical societies. In political liberalism we must distinguish between, first, the political case for intervention based on the public reason of the Law of Peoples and, second, the moral and religious case based on citizens' comprehensive doctrines. In my estimation, the former must prevail if a stable peace is to be maintained among pluralistic societies.

11.3. The Question of Offering Incentives. A genuine question, however, still arises. Should a decent nonliberal society be offered incentives to develop a more liberal democratic constitution? This question raises many difficult issues; I offer a few orienting suggestions. First, it appears clear that an organization of reasonable and decent peoples, such as the United Nations (ideally), should not offer incentives for its member peoples to become more liberal, for this would lead to serious conflicts among its own members. These decent nonliberal peoples themselves, however, may voluntarily request funds for this purpose from, say, an analogue of the IMF (International Monetary Fund), which should treat such funds on the same basis as other loans.

29. See the three aspects of egalitarianism mentioned in *Political Liberalism,* pp. 6–7.

If such a loan were given a special priority, however, that again might arouse conflict between liberal and decent peoples.[30] I also suggest that it is not reasonable for a liberal people to adopt as part of its own foreign policy the granting of subsidies to other peoples as incentives to become more liberal, although persons in civil society may raise private funds for that purpose. It is more important that a liberal democratic government consider what its duty of assistance is to peoples burdened by unfavorable conditions. I shall also argue later (§16) that self-determination, duly constrained by appropriate conditions, is an important good for a people, and that the foreign policy of liberal peoples should recognize that good and not take on the appearance of being coercive. Decent societies should have the opportunity to decide their future for themselves.

§12. Concluding Observations

12.1. Law of Peoples as Universal in Reach. We have now concluded the second part of the ideal theory of the Law of Peoples, the extension of the Law of Peoples to decent hierarchical peoples (§§8–9). I have argued that both reasonably just liberal and decent hierarchical peoples would accept the same Law of Peoples. For this reason, political debate among peoples concerning their mutual relations should be expressed in terms of the content and principles of that law.

In the domestic case, the parties in the original position, in forming the principles of justice, may be described as selecting from classical (or average) utilitarianism, a family of rational intuitionist principles, or a form of moral perfectionism. Political liberalism does not, however, settle upon universal first principles having validity for all parts of moral and political life. The principles of justice for the basic structure of a liberal democratic society are not, that is, fully general principles. They do not apply to all subjects: not to churches or universities, or even to the basic structures of all societies. And they also

---

30. Actually, today's IMF often attaches political conditions to loans, including conditions that do seem to require a move toward more open and liberal democratic institutions.

do not hold for the Law of Peoples, which is autonomous. The eight principles (§4) of the Law of Peoples apply to well-ordered peoples regarded as free and equal; here we may describe the parties as selecting from different interpretations of those eight principles.

In laying out the Law of Peoples, we begin with principles of political justice for the basic structure of a closed and self-contained liberal democratic society.[31] We then model the parties in a second but appropriate original position in which, as representatives of equal peoples, they select the principles of the Law of Peoples for the Society of well-ordered Peoples. The flexibility of the idea of the original position is shown at each step of the procedure by its being modifiable to fit the subject in question. Should the Law of Peoples be reasonably complete, it would include reasonable political principles for all politically relevant subjects: for free and equal citizens and their governments, and for free and equal peoples. It would also include guidelines for forming organizations for cooperation among peoples and for specifying various duties and obligations. If the Law of Peoples is thus reasonably complete, we say that it is "universal in reach," in that it can be extended to give principles for all politically relevant subjects. (The Law of Peoples regulates the most inclusive political subject, the political Society of Peoples.) There is no relevant subject, politically speaking, for which we lack principles and standards to judge. Whether the two-level sequence in Parts I and II is reasonable is settled by whether its outcome can be endorsed on due reflection.[32]

12.2. No Deduction from Practical Reason. Since my presentation of the Law of Peoples is greatly indebted to Kant's idea of the *foedus pacificum* and to so much in his thought, I should say the following: at no point are we deducing the principles of right and justice, or decency, or the principles of rationality, from a conception of practical reason in the background.[33] Rather, we are giving content to an idea

31. See *Political Liberalism,* lecture I, "Fundamental Ideas."

32. I use the phrase to mean the same as "reflective equilibrium" as explained in *A Theory of Justice,* §§3–4, 9.

33. Lecture III of *Political Liberalism* is misleading in this respect. There are many places in that book where I give the impression that the content of the reasonable and the rational is derived from the principles of practical reason.

of practical reason and three of its component parts, the ideas of reasonableness, decency, and rationality. The criteria for these three normative ideas are not deduced, but enumerated and characterized in each case. Practical reason as such is simply reasoning about what to do, or reasoning about what institutions and policies are reasonable, decent, or rational, and why. There is no list of necessary and sufficient conditions for each of these three ideas, and differences of opinion are to be expected. We do conjecture, however, that, if the content of reasonableness, decency, and rationality is laid out properly, the resulting principles and standards of right and justice will hang together and will be affirmed by us on due reflection. Yet there can be no guarantee.

Although the idea of practical reason is associated with Kant, political liberalism is altogether distinct from his transcendental idealism. Political liberalism specifies the idea of the reasonable.[34] The term "reasonable" is often used in *A Theory of Justice,* but not, I think, ever specified. This is done in *Political Liberalism* by giving the relevant criteria for each subject,[35] that is, for each kind of thing to which the term "reasonable" is applied. Thus, reasonable citizens are characterized by their willingness to offer fair terms of social cooperation among equals and by their recognition of the burdens of judgment.[36] In addition, they are said to affirm only reasonable comprehensive doctrines.[37] In turn, such doctrines are reasonable provided they recognize the essentials of a liberal democratic regime[38] and exhibit a reasoned ordering of the many values of life (whether religious or nonreligious) in a coherent and consistent manner. Though these doctrines should be relatively stable, they may evolve in the light of what, given the development of their tradition, are accepted as good and sufficient reasons.[39] It is also reasonable to expect a variety of opinion in political judgments generally, and therefore it is unreasonable to reject all majority voting rules. Otherwise liberal democracy becomes impossible.[40] Po-

34. I refer here to both *Political Liberalism* and "The Idea of Public Reason Revisited."
35. See *Political Liberalism,* p. 94.
36. Ibid., pp. 48–64.
37. Ibid., p. 59.
38. Ibid., p. xviii.
39. Ibid., p. 59.
40. Ibid., p. 393.

litical liberalism offers no way of proving that this specification is it-self reasonable. But none is needed. It is simply politically reasonable to offer fair terms of cooperation to other free and equal citizens, and it is simply politically unreasonable to refuse to do so.

The meaning of the idea of decency is given in the same way. As I have already said, a decent society is not aggressive and engages in war only in self-defense. It has a common good idea of justice that assigns human rights to all its members; its basic structure includes a decent consultation hierarchy that protects these and other rights and ensures that all groups in society are decently represented by elected bodies in the system of consultation. Finally, there must be a sincere and not un-reasonable belief on the part of judges and officials who administer the legal system that the law is indeed guided by a common good idea of justice. Laws supported merely by force are grounds for rebellion and resistance. They are routine in a slave society, but cannot belong to a decent one.

As for the principles of rationality, these are specified in *A Theory of Justice,* which discusses the counting principles of rationality for decid-ing on plans of life, deliberative rationality, and the Aristotelian Prin-ciple.[41] Counting principles are the simplest or most basic principles. They say such things as: other things being equal, it is rational to se-lect the most effective means to one's ends. Or: other things being equal, it is rational to select the more inclusive alternative, the one that enables us to realize all the aims the others do, as well as some addi-tional ends. Again, these principles of rationality are simply specified or worked out, as just illustrated, and not deduced or derived.

41. I write in *A Theory of Justice,* sec. 63, p. 411: "These principles [of rational choice] are to be given by enumeration so that eventually they replace the concept of rationality." On counting principles, see sec. 63, pp. 411–415.

PART III

Nonideal Theory

§13. Just War Doctrine: The Right to War

13.1. Role of Nonideal Theory. To this point we have been concerned with ideal theory. In extending a liberal conception of justice, we have developed an ideal conception of a Law of Peoples for the Society of well-ordered Peoples, that is, liberal and decent peoples. That conception is to guide these well-ordered peoples in their conduct toward one another and in their designing common institutions for their mutual benefit. It is also to guide them in how to deal with non-well-ordered peoples. Before our discussion of the Law of Peoples is complete, we must therefore consider, though we cannot do so wholly adequately, the questions arising from the highly nonideal conditions of our world with its great injustices and widespread social evils. On the assumption that there exist in the world some relatively well-ordered peoples, we ask in nonideal theory how these peoples should act toward non-well-ordered peoples. We take as a basic characteristic of well-ordered peoples that they wish to live in a world in which all peoples accept and follow the (ideal of the) Law of Peoples.

Nonideal theory asks how this long-term goal might be achieved, or worked toward, usually in gradual steps. It looks for policies and courses of action that are morally permissible and politically possible as well as likely to be effective. So conceived, nonideal theory presupposes that ideal theory is already on hand. For until the ideal is identified, at least in outline—and that is all we should expect—nonideal theory lacks an objective, an aim, by reference to which its queries can be answered. Though the specific conditions of our world at any time—the status quo—do not determine the ideal conception of the Society of Peoples, those conditions do affect the specific answers to questions of nonideal theory. For these are questions of transition, of how to work from a world containing outlaw states and societies suffering from unfavorable conditions to a world in which all societies come to accept and follow the Law of Peoples.

There are, as we saw in the Introduction, two kinds of nonideal theory. One kind deals with conditions of noncompliance, that is, with conditions in which certain regimes refuse to comply with a reasonable Law of Peoples; these regimes think a sufficient reason to engage in war is that war advances, or might advance, the regime's rational (not reasonable) interests. These regimes I call *outlaw states*. The other kind of nonideal theory deals with unfavorable conditions, that is, with the conditions of societies whose historical, social, and economic circumstances make their achieving a well-ordered regime, whether liberal or decent, difficult if not impossible. These societies I call *burdened societies*.[1]

I begin with noncompliance theory, and recall that the fifth initial principle of equality (§4.1) of the Law of Peoples gives well-ordered peoples a right to war in self-defense but not, as in the traditional account of sovereignty, a right to war in the rational pursuit of a state's rational interests; these alone are not a sufficient reason. Well-ordered peoples, both liberal and decent, do not initiate war against one another; they go to war only when they sincerely and reasonably believe that their safety and security are seriously endangered by the expan-

---

1. There are also other possibilities. Some states are not well-ordered and violate human rights, but are not aggressive and do not harbor plans to attack their neighbors. They do not suffer from unfavorable conditions, but simply have a state policy that violates the human rights of certain minorities among them. They are therefore outlaw states because they violate what are recognized as rights by the Society of reasonably just and decent Peoples, and they may be subject to some kind of intervention in severe cases. I shall address this matter in more detail in note 6 below and also later in the text.

sionist policies of outlaw states. In what follows, I work out the content of the principles of the Law of Peoples for the conduct of war.

13.2. Well-Ordered Peoples' Right to War. No state has a right to war in the pursuit of its *rational,* as opposed to its *reasonable,* interests. The Law of Peoples does, however, assign to all well-ordered peoples (both liberal and decent), and indeed to any society that follows and honors a reasonably just Law of Peoples, the right to war in self-defense.[2] Although all well-ordered societies have this right, they may interpret their actions in a different way depending on how they think of their ends and purposes. I will note some of these differences.

When a liberal society engages in war in self-defense, it does so to protect and preserve the basic freedoms of its citizens and its constitutionally democratic political institutions. Indeed, a liberal society cannot justly require its citizens to fight in order to gain economic wealth or to acquire natural resources, much less to win power and empire.[3] (When a society pursues these interests, it no longer honors the Law of Peoples, and it becomes an outlaw state.) To trespass on citizens' liberty by conscription, or other such practices in raising armed forces, may only be done on a liberal political conception for the sake of liberty itself, that is, as necessary to defend liberal democratic institutions and civil society's many religious and nonreligious traditions and forms of life.[4]

The special significance of liberal constitutional government is that through its democratic politics, and by following the idea of public reason, citizens can express their conception of their society and take actions appropriate to its defense. That is, ideally, citizens work out a *truly* political opinion, and not simply an opinion about what would best advance their own particular interests, of whatever kind, as members of civil society. Such (truly political) citizens develop an opinion of the rights and wrongs of political right and justice, and of what the well-being of different parts of society requires. As in *Political Liberal-*

2. The right to war normally includes the right to help to defend one's allies.

3. Of course, so-called liberal societies sometimes do this, but that only shows they may act wrongly.

4. See *A Theory of Justice,* sec. 58, pp. 380ff.

ism, each citizen is regarded as having what I have called "the two moral powers"—a capacity for a sense of justice and a capacity for a conception of the good. It is also assumed that each citizen has, at any time, a conception of the good compatible with a comprehensive religious, philosophical, or moral doctrine. These capacities enable citizens to fulfill their role as citizens and underwrite their political and civic autonomy. The principles of justice protect citizens' higher-order interests; these are guaranteed within the framework of the liberal constitution and the basic structure of society. These institutions establish a reasonably just setting within which the background culture[5] of civil society may flourish.

Decent peoples also have a right to war in self-defense. They would describe what they are defending differently from the way a liberal people would; but decent peoples also have something worth defending. For example, the rulers of the imagined decent people, Kazanistan, could rightly defend their decent hierarchical Muslim society. They allow and respect members of different faiths within their society, and they respect the political institutions of other societies, including non-Muslim and liberal societies. They also respect and honor human rights; their basic structure contains a decent consultation hierarchy; and they accept and abide by a (reasonable) Law of Peoples.

The fifth kind of society listed earlier—a *benevolent absolutism*—would also appear to have the right to war in self-defense. While a benevolent absolutism does respect and honor human rights, it is not a well-ordered society, since it does not give its members a meaningful role in making political decisions. But *any* society that is nonaggressive and that honors human rights has the right of self-defense. Its level of spiritual life and culture may not be high in our eyes, but it always has the right to defend itself against invasion of its territory.

13.3. Law of Peoples as Guide to Foreign Policy. A reasonable Law of Peoples guides well-ordered societies in facing outlaw regimes by specifying the aim they are to have in mind and indicating the means they may use or must avoid using. Their defense is, however, only their first

5. See *Political Liberalism,* p. 14.

and most urgent task. Their long-run aim is to bring all societies eventually to honor the Law of Peoples and to become full members in good standing of the society of well-ordered peoples. Human rights would thus be secured everywhere. How to bring all societies to this goal is a question of foreign policy; it calls for political wisdom, and success depends in part on luck. These are not matters to which political philosophy has much to add; I merely recall several familiar points.

For well-ordered peoples to achieve this long-run aim, they should establish new institutions and practices to serve as a kind of confederative center and public forum for their common opinion and policy toward non-well-ordered regimes. They can do this within institutions such as the United Nations or by forming separate alliances of well-ordered peoples on certain issues. This confederative center may be used both to formulate and to express the opinion of the well-ordered societies. There they may expose to public view the unjust and cruel institutions of oppressive and expansionist regimes and their violations of human rights.

Even outlaw regimes are not altogether indifferent to this kind of criticism, especially when the basis of it is a reasonable and well-founded Law of Peoples that cannot be easily dismissed as simply a liberal or Western idea. Gradually over time, then, well-ordered peoples may pressure the outlaw regimes to change their ways; but by itself this pressure is unlikely to be effective. It may need to be backed up by the firm denial of economic and other assistance, or the refusal to admit outlaw regimes as members in good standing in mutually beneficial cooperative practices. What to do on these questions is, however, essentially a matter of political judgment and depends upon a political assessment of the likely consequences of various policies.[6]

6. Earlier I said that we must at some point ask the question whether it is ever legitimate to interfere with outlaw states simply because they violate human rights, even though they are not dangerous and aggressive toward other states, and indeed may be quite weak. Certainly there is a prima facie case for intervention of some kind in such cases, yet one must proceed differently with advanced civilizations than with primitive societies. Primitive, isolated societies, with no contact with liberal or decent societies, we really have no way to influence. But those that are more developed, seeking trade or other cooperative arrangements with liberal or decent societies, are a different story. Imagine a developed society resembling the Aztecs. Although it is harmless to all law-

§14. Just War Doctrine: Conduct of War

14.1. Principles Restricting Conduct of War. Following the above account of the aim of a just war, let us now take up the principles restricting the conduct of war—*jus in bello*. I begin by setting forth six principles and assumptions familiar from traditional thought on the subject:

(i) The aim of a just war waged by a just well-ordered people is a just and lasting peace among peoples, and especially with the people's present enemy.

(ii) Well-ordered peoples do not wage war against each other (§§5, 8), but only against non-well-ordered states whose expansionist aims threaten the security and free institutions of well-ordered regimes and bring about the war.[7]

(iii) In the conduct of war, well-ordered peoples must carefully distinguish three groups: the outlaw state's leaders and officials, its soldiers, and its civilian population. The reason why a well-ordered people must distinguish between an outlaw state's leaders and officials and its civilian population is as follows: since the outlaw state is not well-

abiding members of the Society of Peoples, it holds its own lower class as slaves, keeping the younger members available for human sacrifice in its temples. Is there a tactful approach that could persuade them to cease these practices? I believe they must be made to realize that without honoring human rights, their participation in a system of social cooperation is simply impossible, and that such a system would be to their benefit. A system driven by slavery and the threat of human sacrifice is not a system of cooperation, and cannot be a part of an international system of cooperation. (See also §17.1.) Is there ever a time when forceful intervention might be called for? If the offenses against human rights are egregious and the society does not respond to the imposition of sanctions, such intervention in the defense of human rights would be acceptable and would be called for. Later, in §15.4, I shall discuss further the proposition that in due course, if peoples are exposed to liberal civilization and culture's basic principles and ideals in a positive way, they may become ready to accept and act on them, and violations of human rights may diminish. In that way the circle of mutually caring peoples may expand over time.

7. Responsibility for war rarely falls only on one side. Yet responsibility does admit of degrees. So it is certainly legitimate to assert that one side may bear much heavier responsibility than the other. To put it another way: some hands are dirtier than others. It is also important to recognize that sometimes a well-ordered people with somewhat dirty hands could still have the right and even the duty to go to war to defend itself. This is clear from the history of World War II.

ordered, the civilian members of the society cannot be those who organized and brought on the war.[8] This was done by the leaders and officials, assisted by other elites who control and staff the state apparatus. They are responsible; they willed the war; and, for doing that, they are criminals. But the civilian population, often kept in ignorance and swayed by state propaganda, is not responsible. This is so even if some civilians knew better yet were enthusiastic for the war. No matter what the initial circumstances of war (for instance, the assassination of the heir to the Austro-Hungarian throne, Archduke Ferdinand, by a Serbian nationalist in Sarajevo in June 1914; or the ethnic hatreds in the Balkans and elsewhere today), it is the leaders, and not the common civilians, of nations who finally initiate the war. In view of these principles, both the fire-bombing of Tokyo and other Japanese cities in the spring of 1945 and the atomic bombing of Hiroshima and Nagasaki, all primarily attacks on civilian populations, were very grave wrongs, as they are now widely, though not generally, seen to have been.

As for soldiers of the outlaw state, leaving aside the upper ranks of an officer class, they, like civilians, are not responsible for their state's war. For soldiers are often conscripted and in other ways forced into war; they are coercively indoctrinated in martial virtues; and their patriotism is often cruelly exploited.[9] The reason why they may be at-

---

8. I follow here Michael Walzer's *Just and Unjust Wars* (New York: Basic Books, 1977). This is an impressive work, and what I say does not, I think, depart from it in any significant respect.

9. The Japanese high command fought throughout World War II moved by the spirit of "bushido," the code of honor of the samurai warrior. This code was kept alive by the officers of the Imperial Japanese Army, who in turn indoctrinated the regular Japanese troops into its discipline. Bushido required the soldier to be ready to die rather than be captured, and made surrender punishable by death. Surrender thus being out of the question, every battle became a fight to the death. Japanese soldiers fought to the end in so-called "banzai" attacks (the name comes from the battle cry "Tenno heika banzai": Long live the Emperor) long after they had any chance to fulfill their mission. For example, in the Japanese attack on Bougainville on the Torokina River in March 1944, the Americans lost 78 soldiers, the Japanese more than 5,500. Similar pointless attacks were common, with perhaps the most famous occurring on Saipan in June 1944. The Geneva Conventions for surrender were designed to protect against this. But to defend themselves, the Americans in the South Pacific had no alternative but to fight back in kind, and so normally neither side in infantry engagements (so-called "fire-fights" between small units, squads, platoons, and companies) took prisoners or surrendered. It was the

tacked directly is not that they are responsible for the war, but that well-ordered peoples have no other choice. They cannot defend themselves in any other way, and defend themselves they must.

(iv) Well-ordered peoples must respect, so far as possible, the human rights of the members of the other side, both civilians and soldiers, for two reasons. One is simply that the enemy, like all others, has these rights by the Law of Peoples (§10.3). The other reason is to teach enemy soldiers and civilians the content of those rights by the example set in the treatment they receive. In this way the meaning and significance of human rights are best brought home to them.

(v) Continuing the thought of teaching the content of human rights, the next principle is that well-ordered peoples are by their actions and proclamations, when feasible, to foreshadow during a war both the kind of peace they aim for and the kind of relations they seek. By doing so, they show in an open way the nature of their aims and the kind of people they are. These last duties fall largely on the leaders and officials of the governments of well-ordered peoples, since only they are in the position to speak for the whole people and to act as this principle requires. Although all the preceding principles also specify duties of statesmanship, this is peculiarly true of (iv) and now (v). The way a war is fought and the deeds done in ending it live on in the historical memory of societies and may or may not set the stage for future war. It is always the duty of statesmanship to take this longer view.

(vi) Finally, practical means-end reasoning must always have a restricted role in judging the appropriateness of an action or policy. This mode of thought—whether carried on by utilitarian reasoning, or by cost-benefit analysis, or by weighing national interests, or by other possible ways—must always be framed within and strictly limited by the preceding principles and assumptions. The norms of the conduct

---

duty of the Emperor, had he any sense of his role, to step in and look to the future of his people, and this he eventually did. On the nature of the infantry engagements in the Pacific, so different from those of American troops in France and Germany (leaving aside the Waffen SS), see Eric Bergerud, *Touched with Fire* (New York: Viking, Penguin Books, 1996), pp. 124–145 and 403–425; and Gerald Linderman, *The World within War* (New York: Free Press, 1997), chap. 4. My account of bushido and banzai follows the respective entries in the *Oxford Companion to World War II* (New York: Oxford University Press, 1995), ed. I. C. B. Dear and M. R. D. Foot.

of war set up certain lines we must not cross, so that war plans and strategies and the conduct of battles must lie within the limits they specify. The only exception is in situations of supreme emergency, which I will discuss below.

14.2. Ideal of the Statesman. I have observed that the fourth and fifth principles of the conduct of war are binding especially on statesmen as great leaders of peoples. For they are in the most effective position to represent their people's aims and obligations. But who is the statesman? There is no office of statesman, as there is of president, or chancellor, or prime minister. Rather, the statesman is an ideal, like that of the truthful or virtuous individual. Statesmen are presidents or prime ministers or other high officials who, through their exemplary performance and leadership in their office, manifest strength, wisdom, and courage.[10] They guide their people in turbulent and dangerous times.

The ideal of the statesman is suggested by the saying: the politician looks to the next election, the statesman to the next generation. It is the task of the student of philosophy to articulate and express the permanent conditions and the real interests of a well-ordered society. It is the task of the statesman, however, to discern these conditions and interests in practice. The statesman sees deeper and further than most others and grasps what needs to be done. The statesman must get it right, or nearly so, and then hold fast from this vantage. Washington and Lincoln were statesmen,[11] but Bismarck was not.[12] Statesmen may have their own interests when they hold office, yet they must be selfless in their judgments and assessments of their society's fundamental

10. Kant says in the *Critique of Judgment,* Ak. 262ff., that the courage of the general (*Feldherr*) makes him more sublime than the statesman. Here, however, I believe Kant makes an error of judgment, for the statesman may show courage as much as the general.

11. For Washington, see Stanley Elkins and Eric McKittrick, *The Age of Federalism* (New York: Oxford University Press, 1993), pp. 58–75. For Lincoln, see *Frederick Douglass: Autobiographies,* ed. H. L. Gates (New York: Library of America, 1994); the Oration of 1876 unveiling the Freedmen's monument to Lincoln in Lincoln Park in Washington, D.C., is included as an appendix, pp. 915–925.

12. See my comment in Part I, §5.5, note 67.

interests and must not be swayed, especially in war, by passions of vindictiveness.[13]

Above all, statesmen are to hold fast to the aim of gaining a just peace, and they are to avoid the things that make achieving such a peace more difficult. In this regard, they must assure that the proclamations made on behalf of their people make clear that once peace is securely reestablished, the enemy society is to be granted an autonomous well-ordered regime of its own. (For a time, however, limits may be rightly placed on the defeated society's freedom in foreign policy.)

The enemy's people are not to be held as slaves or serfs after surrender,[14] or denied in due time their full liberties. Thus, the ideal of the statesman includes moral elements. Merely acting in so-called world-historical ways does not make someone a statesman. Napoleon and Hitler incalculably altered history and human life; but statesmen they decidedly were not.

14.3. Supreme Emergency Exemption. This exemption[15] allows us to set aside—in certain special circumstances—the strict status of civilians that normally prevents their being directly attacked in war. We must proceed here with caution. Were there times during World War II when Britain could properly have held that civilians' strict status was suspended, and thus could have bombed Hamburg or Berlin? Possibly, but only if it was sure that the bombing would have done some substantial good; such action cannot be justified by a doubtful marginal gain.[16] When Britain was alone and had no other means to break Germany's superior power, the bombing of German cities was arguably justifiable.[17] This period extended, at the least, from the fall of France in June 1940 until Russia had clearly beaten off the first German assault in the summer and fall of 1941 and showed that it would be able

13. A remarkable aspect of Lincoln is his selflessness as a statesman.
14. See Churchill's remarks explaining the meaning of "unconditional surrender" in *The Hinge of Fate* (Boston: Houghton Mifflin, 1950), pp. 685–688.
15. The name "supreme emergency" is from Walzer, in *Just and Unjust Wars,* chap. 16, pp. 255–265.
16. I have benefited here from discussion with Thomas Pogge.
17. Prohibitions such as that against the torture of prisoners of war still remain in place.

to fight Germany until the end. It could be argued that this period extended further until the summer and fall of 1942 or even through the Battle of Stalingrad (which ended with German surrender in February 1943). But the bombing of Dresden in February 1945 was clearly too late.

Whether the supreme emergency exemption applies depends upon certain circumstances, about which judgments will sometimes differ. Britain's bombing of Germany until the end of 1941 or 1942 could be justified because Germany could not be allowed to win the war, and this for two basic reasons. First, Nazism portended incalculable moral and political evil for civilized life everywhere. Second, the nature and history of constitutional democracy and its place in European history were at stake. Churchill really did not exaggerate when he said to the House of Commons on the day France capitulated that, "if we fail [to stand up to Hitler], the whole world including the United States . . . will sink into a new Dark Age." This kind of threat, in sum, justifies invoking the supreme emergency exemption, on behalf not only of constitutional democracies, but of all well-ordered societies.

The peculiar evil of Nazism needs to be understood. It was characteristic of Hitler that he recognized no possibility at all of a political relationship with his enemies. They were always to be cowed by terror and brutality, and ruled by force.[18] From the beginning, the campaign against Russia was to be a war of destruction and even at times extermination of Slavic peoples, with the original inhabitants remaining, if at all, only as serfs. When Goebbels and others protested that the war could not be won that way, Hitler refused to listen.[19]

14.4. Failure of Statesmanship. It is clear, however, that the supreme emergency exemption never held at any time for the United States in its war with Japan. The United States was not justified in fire-bomb-

18. See Stuart Hampshire's instructive discussion of this in *Innocence and Experience* (Cambridge, Mass.: Harvard University Press, 1989), pp. 66–78.

19. On Goebbels's and others' protests, see Alan Bullock, *Hitler: A Study in Tyranny* (London: Oldham's Press, 1952), pp. 633–644. See also Omar Bartov, *Hitler's Army* (New York: Oxford University Press, 1991). This work studies the descent into brutality and barbarism of the war on the Eastern Front where the Wehrmacht was defeated.

ing Japanese cities; and during the discussion among allied leaders in June and July 1945 prior to the use of the atomic bomb on Hiroshima and Nagasaki, the weight of practical means-end reasoning carried the day, overwhelming the qualms of those who felt that limits were being crossed.

Dropping the bombs, it was claimed, was justified in order to hasten the end of the war. It is clear that Truman and most other allied leaders thought it would do that and thereby save the lives of American soldiers. Japanese lives, military and civilian, presumably counted for less. Moreover, dropping the bombs, it was reasoned, would give the Emperor and the Japanese leaders a way to save face, an important matter given Japanese military samurai culture. Some scholars also believe the bombs were dropped in order to impress Russia with American power and make Russian leaders more agreeable to American demands.[20]

The failure of all these reasons to justify violations of the principles for the conduct of war is evident. What caused this failure of statesmanship on the part of allied leaders? Truman once described the Japanese as beasts and said they should be treated as such;[21] yet how foolish it sounds now to call the Germans and the Japanese as a whole barbarians and beasts.[22] The Nazis and Tojo militarists, yes, but they

20. See Gar Alperovitz, *Atomic Diplomacy: Hiroshima and Potsdam* (New York: Penguin Books, 1985), for discussion of this last reason. If true, it is particularly damning. I make no attempt to estimate the relative importance given these reasons.

21. See David McCullough's *Truman* (New York: Simon and Schuster, 1992), p. 458, for the exchange between Truman and Senator Russell of Georgia in August 1945.

22. Daniel Goldhagen's *Hitler's Willing Executioners: Ordinary Germans and the Holocaust* (New York: Knopf, 1996) gives, I think, the wrong view of the Holocaust. It did not originate as he claims in a cognitive mind-set peculiar to German political culture that had existed for centuries and to which the Nazis simply gave expression. While anti-semitism had been present in Germany, it had also been present throughout most of Europe—in France (witness the Dreyfus case in the late nineteenth century) as well as pogroms in Poland and Russia, and it became church policy to isolate Jews in ghettos during the Counter Reformation in the late sixteenth century. The lesson of the Holocaust is, rather, that a charismatic leader of a powerful totalitarian and militaristic state can, with incessant and rabid propaganda, incite a sufficient number of the population to carry out even enormously and hideously evil plans. The Holocaust might have happened anywhere such a state came to be. Moreover, not all Germans succumbed to

are not the German and Japanese people. Churchill ascribed his failure of judgment in bombing Dresden to the passion and intensity of the conflict.[23] But it is a duty of statesmanship to prevent such feelings, as natural and inevitable as they may be, from altering the course a well-ordered people should follow in striving for peace. The statesman understands that relations with the present enemy have special importance: war must be openly and publicly conducted in ways that prepare the enemy people for how they will be treated and that make a lasting and amicable peace possible. The fears or fantasies on the part of the enemy people that they will be subject to revenge and retaliation must be put to rest. Difficult though it may be, the present enemy must be seen as a future associate in a shared and just peace.

Another failure of statesmanship was in not considering negotiations with the Japanese before any drastic steps such as the fire-bombing of Japanese cities in the spring of 1945 and the bombing of Hiroshima and Nagasaki were taken. I believe this route could have been effective and avoided further casualties. An invasion was unnecessary by August 6, as the war was effectively over.[24] But whether that is true or not makes no difference. As a liberal democratic people, the United States owed the Japanese people an offer of negotiations in order to end the war. Their government and military had been instructed by the Emperor on June 26,[25] and perhaps earlier, to look for a way to end the war, and they surely must have realized that, with their navy destroyed and the outer and inner islands taken, the war was lost. The leaders of the regime, imbued with the samurai code of honor, would not have considered negotiations on their own, but under the Emperor's instructions they might have reacted positively to American overtures. But these never came.

Hitler's invective, and why some people did cannot be explained simply by native anti-semitism. See also *Unwilling Germans? The Goldhagen Debate,* ed. Robert R. Shandley, trans. Jeremiah Riemer (Minneapolis: University of Minnesota Press, 1998) for reviews and discussions of Goldhagen's book by a number of contemporary German writers.

23. See Martin Gilbert, *Winston Churchill: Never Despair,* vol. 8 (Boston: Houghton Mifflin, 1988), p. 259.

24. See Barton Bernstein, "The Atomic Bombings Reconsidered," *Foreign Affairs,* 74:1, January–February 1995.

25. See Gerhard Weinberg, *A World at Arms* (Cambridge: Cambridge University Press, 1994), pp. 886–889.

14.5. Significance of Political Culture. It is clear that the bombings
of Hiroshima and Nagasaki and the fire-bombing of Japanese cities
were great wrongs of the kind that the duties of statesmanship require
political leaders to avoid; yet it is equally clear that an articulate expression of the principles of just war, if introduced at that time, would
not have altered the outcome. For it was simply too late: by that time
the bombing of civilians had become an accepted practice of war. Reflections on just war would have fallen on deaf ears. For this reason,
these questions must be carefully considered in advance of conflict.

Similarly, the grounds of constitutional democracy and the basis of
its rights and duties need to be continually discussed in all the many
associations of civil society as part of citizens' understanding and education prior to taking part in political life. These matters need to be
part of the political culture; they should not dominate the day-to-day
contents of ordinary politics, but must be presupposed and operating
in the background. At the time of the World War II bombings, there
was not sufficient prior grasp of the great importance of the principles
of just war for the expression of them to have blocked the handy appeal to practical means-end reasoning. This reasoning justifies too
much, too quickly, and provides a way for the dominant forces in government to quiet any bothersome moral scruples. If the principles of
war are not put forward before that time, they simply become more
considerations to be balanced in the scales. These principles must be
in place well in advance of war and widely understood by citizens generally. The failure of statesmanship rests in part on and is compounded
by the failure of the public political culture—including its military's
culture and its doctrine of war[26]—to respect the principles of just war.

26. A great temptation to evil is airpower. Oddly enough, the official military doctrine of the Luftwaffe had it right (if for the wrong reason): airpower is to support the
army and navy in the field and on the sea. Proper military doctrine declares that airpower must not be used to attack civilians. Following this doctrine would not, I think,
have affected the effectiveness of the American Army and Navy in defeating the Japanese. The Navy defeated the Japanese navy at Midway in June of 1942, defeated its car-
rier fleet in the battle of the Philippine Sea off Saipan in June 1944, and crippled its
battle fleet in San Bernadino Strait north of Leyte and in the Suriago Strait to the south
of Leyte in October 1944; while the Marines took the Marshalls, Guam, Saipan, and
Iwo Jima, and the Army took New Guinea and the Philippines ending with the battle
for Okinawa. That effectively marked the end of war. Indeed, the stage for a negotiated
peace had been set well before that.

Two nihilist doctrines of war are to be repudiated absolutely. One is expressed by Sherman's remark, "War is hell," with the implication that anything goes to get it over with as soon as possible.[27] The other holds that we are all guilty, so we stand on the same level and cannot rightly blame or be blamed. These doctrines—if they deserve this title—both superficially deny all reasonable distinctions; their moral emptiness is manifest in the fact that just and decent civilized societies—their institutions and laws, their civil life, background culture, and mores—depend always on making significant moral and political distinctions. Certainly war is a kind of hell; but why should that mean that normative distinctions cease to hold? Granted also that sometimes all or nearly all may be to some degree guilty; but that does not mean that all are equally so. In short, there is never a time when we are excused from the fine-grained distinctions of moral and political principles and graduated restraints.[28]

14.6. Comparison with Christian Doctrine. The Law of Peoples is both similar to and different from the familiar Christian natural law doctrine of just war.[29] They are similar in that both imply that universal peace among nations is possible, if all peoples act according to either the Christian natural law doctrine *or* the Law of Peoples, which does not preclude the natural law or any other reasonable comprehensive doctrine.

However, it is important here to take a step back and to see where

27. In justice to Sherman, it must be said that on his march through Georgia in the fall of 1864 his troops only destroyed property. They did not attack civilians.

28. See Hannah Arendt's *Eichmann in Jerusalem* (New York: Viking Press, 1963), especially the last four pages of the Postscript on the role of judgment.

29. This doctrine originates from Saint Ambrose and Saint Augustine, who drew on the classical writers of Greece and Rome. Roland Bainton's *Christian Attitudes toward War and Peace* (Nashville: Abingdon Press, 1960) provides a useful summary of Augustine on pp. 91–100. Augustine produced no treatise or sustained discussion of his views, so they must be gathered from his many writings. See also St. Thomas Aquinas, *Summa Theologica*, II-II, Question 40, Articles 1–4; and Francisco de Vitoria, "On the Law of War," in *Political Writings*, ed. A. Pagden and J. Lawrence (Cambridge: Cambridge University Press, 1991), pp. 295–327. Ralph Potter provides a general discussion of Christian doctrine with bibliographical comments and references in his *War and Moral Discourse* (Richmond: John Knox Press, 1969). For a useful survey of the ancient world, see Doyne Dawson, *The Origins of Western Warfare* (Boulder: The Westview Press, 1996).

the essential difference lies between the Law of Peoples and the natural law; that is, in how they are conceived. The natural law is thought to be part of the law of God that can be known through the natural powers of reason by our study of the structure of the world. As God has supreme authority over all creation, this law is binding for all humankind as members of one community. Thus understood, the natural law is distinct from the eternal law, which lies in God's reason and guides God's activity in creating and sustaining the world. The natural law is also distinct from the revealed law, which cannot be known by the powers of natural reason, and from ecclesiastical law, which applies to religious and jurisdictional matters of the church. By contrast, the Law of Peoples falls within the domain of the political as a political conception. That is, though the Law of Peoples could be supported by the Christian doctrine of natural law, its principles are expressed solely in terms of a political conception and its political values.[30] Both views support the right to war in self-defense; but the content of the principles for the conduct of war is not in all ways the same.

This last remark is illustrated by the Catholic doctrine of double-effect. It agrees with the principles of the Law of Peoples for the conduct of war (as set out above in §14.1) that civilians are not to be directly attacked. Both views agree also that the fire-bombing of Japan in the spring and summer of 1945 and the bombing of Hiroshima and Nagasaki were great wrongs. Yet they differ in that the principles for the conduct of war in the social contract conception include the supreme emergency exemption (§14.3), but the doctrine of double-effect does not. The doctrine of double-effect forbids civilian casualties except insofar as they are the unintended and indirect result of a legitimate attack on a military target. Resting on the divine command that the innocent must never be killed, this doctrine says that one must never act with the intention of attacking the enemy state by the means of taking the innocent

30. I should note here that, although the Law of Peoples, like political liberalism, is strictly political, it is *not* secular. By this I mean that it does not deny religious or other values, say through some "non-theistic" or "non-metaphysical" (social or natural) theory. It is for citizens and statesmen to decide, in the light of their comprehensive doctrines, the weight of political values. For further discussion, see *Political Liberalism*, IX, "Reply to Habermas," §2, pp. 385–395, and "The Idea of Public Reason Revisited," §6.

lives of its civilians. Political liberalism allows the supreme emergency exemption; the Catholic doctrine rejects it, saying that we must have faith and adhere to God's command.[31] This is intelligible doctrine but is contrary to the duties of the statesman in political liberalism.

The statesman, discussed in §14.2, is a central figure in considering the conduct of war, and must be prepared to wage a just war in defense of liberal democratic regimes. Indeed, citizens expect those who seek the office of president or prime minister to do so, and it would violate a fundamental political understanding, at least in the absence of a clear public declaration prior to election, to refuse to do so for religious, philosophical, or moral reasons. Quakers, who oppose all war, can join an overlapping consensus on a constitutional regime, but they cannot always endorse a democracy's particular decisions—here, to engage in a war of self-defense—even when those decisions are reasonable in the light of its political values. This indicates that they could not in good faith, in the absence of special circumstances, seek the highest offices in a liberal democratic regime. The statesman must look to the political world, and must, in extreme cases, be able to distinguish between the interests of the well-ordered regime he or she serves and the dictates of the religious, philosophical, or moral doctrine that he or she personally lives by.

§15. Burdened Societies

15.1. Unfavorable Conditions. In noncompliance theory we have seen that the long-term goal of (relatively) well-ordered societies is somehow to bring the outlaw states into the Society of well-ordered Peoples. The outlaw states[32] of modern Europe in the early modern

---

31. See the powerful essay by G. E. M. Anscombe, "War and Murder," in *Nuclear Weapons and Christian Conscience,* ed. Walter Stein (London: Merlin Press, 1961), pp. 45–62. This was written to object to Oxford's decision to award an honorary degree to President Truman in 1952. The view in §14 agrees with Anscombe in the particular case of Hiroshima.

32. Some may object to this term, yet these states were indeed outlaw societies. Their wars were essentially dynastic wars to which the lives and fundamental interests of most members of the societies were sacrificed.

period—Spain, France, and the Hapsburgs—or, more recently, Germany, all tried at one time to subject much of Europe to their will. They hoped to spread their religion and culture and sought dominion and glory, not to mention wealth and territory. These states were among the more effectively organized and economically advanced societies of their day. Their fault lay in their political traditions and institutions of law, property, and class structure, with their sustaining religious and moral beliefs and underlying culture. It is these things that shape a society's political will; and they are the elements that must change before a society can support a reasonable Law of Peoples.

In what follows I take up the second kind of nonideal theory, namely, societies burdened by unfavorable conditions (henceforth, *burdened societies*). Burdened societies, while they are not expansive or aggressive, lack the political and cultural traditions, the human capital and know-how, and, often, the material and technological resources needed to be well-ordered. The long-term goal of (relatively) well-ordered societies should be to bring burdened societies, like outlaw states, into the Society of well-ordered Peoples. Well-ordered peoples have a *duty* to assist burdened societies. It does not follow, however, that the only way, or the best way, to carry out this duty of assistance is by following a principle of distributive justice to regulate economic and social inequalities among societies. Most such principles do not have a defined goal, aim, or cut-off point, beyond which aid may cease.

The levels of wealth and welfare among societies may vary, and presumably do so; but adjusting those levels is not the object of the duty of assistance. Only burdened societies need help. Furthermore, not all such societies are poor, any more than all well-ordered societies are wealthy. A society with few natural resources and little wealth can be well-ordered if its political traditions, law, and property and class structure with their underlying religious and moral beliefs and culture are such as to sustain a liberal or decent society.

15.2. First Guideline for Duty of Assistance. The first guideline to consider is that a well-ordered society need not be a wealthy society. I recall here three basic points about the principle of "just savings" (within a domestic society) as I elaborated it in *A Theory of Justice*, §44.

(a) The purpose of a just (real) savings principle is to establish (reasonably) just basic institutions for a free constitutional democratic society (or any well-ordered society) and to secure a social world that makes possible a worthwhile life for all its citizens.

(b) Accordingly, savings may stop once just (or decent) basic institutions have been established. At this point real saving (that is, net additions to real capital of all kinds) may fall to zero; and existing stock only needs to be maintained, or replaced, and nonrenewable resources carefully husbanded for future use as appropriate. Thus, the savings rate as a constraint on current consumption is to be expressed in terms of aggregate capital accumulated, resource use forgone, and technology developed to conserve and regenerate the capacity of the natural world to sustain its human population. With these and other essential elements tallied in, a society may, of course, continue to save after this point, but it is no longer a duty of justice to do so.

(c) Great wealth is not necessary to establish just (or decent) institutions. How much is needed will depend on a society's particular history as well as on its conception of justice. Thus the levels of wealth among well-ordered peoples will not, in general, be the same.

These three features of the savings process discussed in *A Theory of Justice* bring out the similarity between the duty of assistance in the Law of Peoples and the duty of just savings in the domestic case. In each instance, the aim is to realize and preserve just (or decent) institutions, and not simply to increase, much less to maximize indefinitely, the average level of wealth, or the wealth of any society or any particular class in society. In these respects the duty of assistance and the duty of just savings express the same underlying idea.[33]

---

33. The main idea I express here draws on J. S. Mill's *The Principles of Political Economy*, 1st ed. (London, 1848), book IV, chap. 6, "The Stationary State." I follow Mill's view that the purpose of saving is to make possible a just basic structure of society; once that is safely secured, real saving (net increase in real capital) may no longer be necessary. "The art of living" is more important than "the art of getting on," to use his words. The thought that real saving and economic growth are to go on indefinitely, upwards and onwards, with no specified goal in sight, is the idea of the business class of a capitalist society. But what counts for Mill are just basic institutions and the well-being of what Mill would call "the labouring class." Mill says: ". . . the decision [between a just system of private property and socialism] will depend mainly on one consideration,

15.3. Second Guideline. A second guideline for thinking about how to carry out the duty of assistance is to realize that the political culture of a burdened society is all-important; and that, at the same time, there is no recipe, certainly no easy recipe, for well-ordered peoples to help a burdened society to change its political and social culture. I believe that the causes of the wealth of a people and the forms it takes lie in their political culture and in the religious, philosophical, and moral traditions that support the basic structure of their political and social institutions, as well as in the industriousness and cooperative talents of its members, all supported by their political virtues. I would further conjecture that there is no society anywhere in the world—except for marginal cases[34]—with resources so scarce that it could not, were it reasonably and rationally organized and governed, become well-ordered. Historical examples seem to indicate that resource-poor countries may do very well (e.g., Japan), while resource-rich countries may have serious difficulties (e.g., Argentina). The crucial elements that make the difference are the political culture, the political virtues and civic society of the country, its members' probity and industriousness, their capacity for innovation, and much else. Crucial also is the country's population policy: it must take care that it does not overburden its lands and economy with a larger population than it can sustain. But one way or the other, the duty of assistance is in no way diminished. What must be realized is that merely dispensing funds will not suffice to rectify basic political and social injustices (though money is often

---

viz., which of the two systems is consistent with the greatest amount of human liberty and spontaneity. After the means of subsistence are assured, the next in strength of personal wants of human beings is liberty, and (unlike physical wants which as civilization advances become more moderate and more amenable to control) it increases instead of diminishing in intensity as intelligence and the moral faculties are more developed." From the 7th and last edition of the *Principles* published in Mill's lifetime, paragraph 9 of §3 of chap. 1 of book II. What Mill says here is perfectly consistent with the Law of Peoples and its structure of political values, though I could not accept it as it stands. References to Mill's *Principles* are from the paperback edition, edited by Jonathan Riley, in Oxford World Classics (Oxford: Oxford University Press, 1994). The complete text of the *Principles* is now in *The Complete Works of John Stuart Mill,* vols. 2 and 3, Introduction by V. W. Bladen, ed. J. M. Robson (London: University of Toronto Press, Routledge and Kegan Paul, 1965).

34. Arctic Eskimos, for example, are rare enough, and need not affect our general approach. I assume their problems could be handled in an *ad hoc* way.

essential). But an emphasis on human rights may work to change ineffective regimes and the conduct of the rulers who have been callous about the well-being of their own people.

This insistence on human rights is supported by Amartya Sen's work on famines.[35] In his empirical study of four well-known historical cases (Bengal, 1943; Ethiopia, 1972–1974; Sahel, 1972–1973; and Bangladesh, 1974), he found that food decline need not be the main cause of famine, or even a minor cause. In the cases he studied, the drop in food production was not great enough to lead to famine given a decent government that cared for the well-being of all its people and had in place a reasonable scheme of backup entitlements provided through public institutions. The main problem was the failure of the respective governments to distribute (and supplement) what food there was. Sen concluded: "famines are economic disasters, not just food crises."[36] In other words, they are attributable to faults within the political and social structure, and its failure to institute policies to remedy the effects of shortfalls in food production. A government's allowing people to starve when it is preventable reflects a lack of concern for human rights, and well-ordered regimes as I have described them will not allow this to happen. Insisting on human rights will, it is to be hoped, help to prevent famines from developing, and will exert pressure in the direction of effective governments in a well-ordered Society of Peoples. (I note, by the way, that there would be massive starvation in every Western democracy were there no schemes in place to help the unemployed.)

Respecting human rights could also relieve population pressure within a burdened society, relative to what the economy of the society can decently sustain.[37] A decisive factor here appears to be the status

---

35. See Amartya Sen, *Poverty and Famines* (Oxford: Clarendon Press, 1981). Sen's book with Jean Drèze, *Hunger and Public Action* (Oxford: Clarendon Press, 1989), confirms these points and stresses the success of democratic regimes in coping with poverty and hunger. See their summary statement in chap. 13, p. 25. See also the important work of Partha Dasgupta, *An Inquiry into Well-Being and Destitution* (Oxford: Clarendon Press, 1993), chaps. 1, 2, and 5.

36. Sen, *Poverty and Famines,* p. 162.

37. I do not use the term "overpopulation" here since it seems to imply the idea of optimal population; but what is that? When seen as relative to what the economy can sustain, whether there is population pressure is a clear enough question. I am indebted to Amartya Sen on this point.

of women. Some societies—China is a familiar example—have imposed harsh restrictions on the size of families and have adopted other draconian measures. But there is no need to be so harsh. The simplest, most effective, most acceptable policy is to establish the elements of equal justice for women. Instructive here is the Indian state of Kerala, which in the late 1970s empowered women to vote and to participate in politics, to receive and use education, and to own and manage wealth and property. As a result, within several years Kerala's birth rate fell below China's, without invoking the coercive powers of the state.[38] Like policies have been instituted elsewhere—for example, in Bangladesh, Colombia, and Brazil—with similar results. The elements of basic justice have proven themselves essential for sound social policy. Injustice is supported by deep-seated interests and will not easily disappear; but it cannot excuse itself by pleading lack of natural resources.

To repeat, there is no easy recipe for helping a burdened society to change its political culture. Throwing funds at it is usually undesirable, and the use of force is ruled out by the Law of Peoples. But certain kinds of advice may be helpful, and burdened societies would do well to pay particular attention to the fundamental interests of women. The fact that women's status is often founded on religion, or bears a close relation to religious views,[39] is not in itself the cause of their subjection, since other causes are usually present. One may explain that all kinds of well-ordered societies affirm human rights and have at least the features of a decent consultation hierarchy or its analogue. These features require that any group representing women's fundamental interests must include a majority of women (§8.3). The idea is that any conditions of the consultation procedure that are necessary to prevent violations of the human rights of women are to be adopted. This is not a peculiarly liberal idea but one that is also common to all decent peoples.

38. See Amartya Sen, "Population: Delusion and Reality," *The New York Review of Books*, September 22, 1994, pp. 62–71. On Kerala, see pp. 70ff. China's birth rate in 1979 was 2.8; Kerala's 3.0. In 1991 these rates were 2.0 and 1.8 respectively.

39. I say this because many Muslim writers deny that Islam sanctions the inequality of women in many Muslim societies, and attribute it to various historical causes. See Leila Ahmed, *Women and Gender in Islam* (New Haven: Yale University Press, 1992).

We can, then, bring this idea to bear as a condition on offered assistance without being subject to the charge of improperly undermining a society's religion and culture. The principle here is similar to one that is always followed in regard to the claims of religion. Thus, a religion cannot claim as a justification that its intolerance of other religions is necessary for it to maintain itself. In the same way a religion cannot claim as a justification for its subjection of women that it is necessary for its survival. Basic human rights are involved, and these belong to the common institutions and practices of all liberal and decent societies.[40]

15.4. Third Guideline. The third guideline for carrying out the duty of assistance is that its aim is to help burdened societies to be able to manage their own affairs reasonably and rationally and eventually to become members of the Society of well-ordered Peoples. This defines the "target" of assistance. After it is achieved, further assistance is not required, even though the now well-ordered society may still be relatively poor. Thus the well-ordered societies giving assistance must not act paternalistically, but in measured ways that do not conflict with the final aim of assistance: freedom and equality for the formerly burdened societies.

Leaving aside the deep question of whether some forms of culture and ways of life are good in themselves, as I believe they are, it is surely a good for individuals and associations to be attached to their particular culture and to take part in its common public and civic life. In this way belonging to a particular political society, and being at home in its civic and social world, gains expression and fulfillment.[41] This is no small thing. It argues for preserving significant room for the idea of a people's self-determination and for some kind of loose or confederative form of a Society of Peoples, provided the divisive hostilities of different cultures can be tamed, as it seems they can be, by a society of well-ordered regimes. We seek a world in which ethnic hatreds leading to nationalistic wars will have ceased. A proper patriotism (§5.2) is an

40. See *Political Liberalism,* V: §6.
41. Ibid., V: §7.

attachment to one's people and country, and a willingness to defend its legitimate claims while fully respecting the legitimate claims of other peoples.[42] Well-ordered peoples should try to encourage such regimes.

15.5. Duty of Assistance and Affinity. A legitimate concern about the duty of assistance is whether the motivational support for following it presupposes a degree of affinity among peoples, that is, a sense of social cohesion and closeness, that cannot be expected even in a society of liberal peoples—not to mention in a society of all well-ordered peoples—with their separate languages, religions, and cultures. The members of a single domestic society share a common central government and political culture, and the moral learning of political concepts and principles works most effectively in the context of society-wide political and social institutions that are part of their shared daily life.[43] Taking part in shared institutions every day, members of the same society should be able to resolve political conflicts and problems within the society on a common basis in terms of public reason.

It is the task of the statesman to struggle against the potential lack of affinity among different peoples and try to heal its causes insofar as they derive from past domestic institutional injustices, and from the hostility among social classes inherited through their common history and antagonisms. Since the affinity among peoples is naturally weaker (as a matter of human psychology) as society-wide institutions include a larger area and cultural distances increase, the statesman must continually combat these shortsighted tendencies.[44]

What encourages the statesman's work is that relations of affinity are not a fixed thing, but may continually grow stronger over time as peoples come to work together in cooperative institutions they have de-

42. These are specified by the Law of Peoples.

43. Joshua Cohen, "A More Democratic Liberalism," *Michigan Law Review,* vol. 92, no. 6 (May 1994), pp. 1532–33.

44. Here I draw on a psychological principle that social learning of moral attitudes supporting political institutions works most effectively through society-wide shared institutions and practices. The learning weakens under the conditions mentioned in the text. In a realistic utopia this psychological principle sets limits to what can sensibly be proposed as the content of the Law of Peoples.

veloped. It is characteristic of liberal and decent peoples that they seek a world in which all peoples have a well-ordered regime. At first we may suppose this aim is moved by each people's *self-interest,* for such regimes are not dangerous but peaceful and cooperative. Yet as cooperation between peoples proceeds apace they may come to care about each other, and affinity between them becomes stronger. Hence, they are no longer moved simply by self-interest but by mutual concern for each other's way of life and culture, and they become willing to make sacrifices for each other. This mutual caring is the outcome of their fruitful cooperative efforts and common experiences over a considerable period of time.

The relatively narrow circle of mutually caring peoples in the world today may expand over time and must never be viewed as fixed. Gradually, peoples are no longer moved by self-interest alone or by their mutual caring alone, but come to affirm their liberal and decent civilization and culture, until eventually they become ready to act on the *ideals and principles* their civilization specifies. Religious toleration has historically first appeared as a *modus vivendi* between hostile faiths, later becoming a moral principle shared by civilized peoples and recognized by their leading religions. The same is true of the abolition of slavery and serfdom, the rule of law, the right to war only in self-defense, and the guarantee of human rights. These become ideals and principles of liberal and decent civilizations, and principles of the Law of all civilized Peoples.

§16. On Distributive Justice among Peoples

16.1. Equality among Peoples. There are two views about this. One holds that equality is just, or a good in itself. The Law of Peoples, on the other hand, holds that inequalities are not always unjust, and that when they are, it is because of their unjust effects on the basic structure of the Society of Peoples, and on relations among peoples and among their members.[45] We saw the great importance of this basic

45. My discussion of inequality is greatly indebted, as so often, to T. M. Scanlon.

structure when discussing the need for toleration of decent nonliberal peoples (§§7.2–7.3).

I note three reasons for being concerned with inequality in domestic society and consider how each applies to the Society of Peoples. One reason for reducing inequalities within a domestic society is to relieve the suffering and hardships of the poor. Yet this does not require that all persons be equal in wealth. In itself, it doesn't matter how great the gap between rich and poor may be. What matters are the consequences. In a liberal domestic society that gap cannot be wider than the criterion of reciprocity allows, so that the least advantaged (as the third liberal principle requires) have sufficient all-purpose means to make intelligent and effective use of their freedoms and to lead reasonable and worthwhile lives. When that situation exists, there is no further need to narrow the gap. Similarly, in the basic structure of the Society of Peoples, once the duty of assistance is satisfied and all peoples have a working liberal or decent government, there is again no reason to narrow the gap between the average wealth of different peoples.

A second reason for narrowing the gap between rich and poor within a domestic society is that such a gap often leads to some citizens being stigmatized and treated as inferiors, and that is unjust. Thus, in a liberal or decent society, conventions that establish ranks to be recognized socially by expressions of deference must be guarded against. They may unjustly wound the self-respect of those not so recognized. The same would be true of the basic structure of the Society of Peoples should citizens in one country feel inferior to the citizens of another because of its greater riches, *provided* that those feelings are justified. Yet when the duty of assistance is fulfilled, and each people has its own liberal or decent government, these feelings are unjustified. For then each people adjusts the significance and importance of the wealth of its own society for itself. If it is not satisfied, it can continue to increase savings, or, if that is not feasible, borrow from other members of the Society of Peoples.

A third reason for considering the inequalities among peoples concerns the important role of fairness in the political processes of the basic structure of the Society of Peoples. In the domestic case this concern is evident in securing the fairness of elections and of political opportunities to run for public office. Public financing of political parties and campaigns tries to address these matters. Also, when we speak of fair equality of opportunity, more than formal legal equality is meant. We mean roughly that background social conditions are such that each citizen, regardless of class or origin, should have the same chance of attaining a favored social position, given the same talents and willingness to try. Policies for achieving this fair equality of opportunity include, for example, securing fair education for all and eliminating unjust discrimination. Fairness also plays an important role in the political processes of the basic structure of the Society of Peoples, analogous to, though not the same as, its role in the domestic case.

Basic fairness among peoples is given by their being represented equally in the second original position with its veil of ignorance. Thus the representatives of peoples will want to preserve the independence of their own society and its equality in relation to others. In the working of organizations and loose confederations of peoples, inequalities are designed to serve the many ends that peoples share (§4.5). In this case the larger and smaller peoples will be ready to make larger and smaller contributions and to accept proportionately larger and smaller returns. In addition, the parties will formulate guidelines for setting up cooperative organizations, and will agree to standards of fairness for trade as well as to certain provisions for mutual assistance. Should these cooperative organizations have unjustified distributive effects, these would have to be corrected in the basic structure of the Society of Peoples.

16.2. Distributive Justice among Peoples. Several principles have been proposed to regulate inequalities among peoples and prevent their becoming excessive. Two of these are discussed by Charles Beitz.[46] Another is Thomas Pogge's Egalitarian Principle,[47] which is similar in many respects to Beitz's second principle of redistributive justice.

---

46. Charles Beitz, *Political Theory and International Relations* (Princeton: Princeton Univerity Press, 1979).

47. Pogge's global egalitarian principle as set out in "An Egalitarian Law of Peoples," PAPA, 23:3 (Summer 1994) is not a statement of his own preferred view, but one that he sees as internal to *A Theory of Justice*. It states how he thinks the international system should be treated if it were treated as the domestic one is treated in *A Theory of Justice*.

These are suggestive and much-discussed principles, and I need to say why I don't accept them. But, of course, I do accept Beitz's and Pogge's goals of attaining liberal or decent institutions, securing human rights, and meeting basic needs. These I believe are covered by the duty of assistance discussed in the preceding section.

First let me state Beitz's two principles. He distinguishes between what he calls "the resource redistribution principle" and a "global distribution principle." The distinction between them is as follows: suppose first, that the production of goods and services in all countries is *autarkic,* that is, each country relies entirely on its own labor and resources without trade of any kind. Beitz holds that some areas have ample resources, and societies in such areas can be expected to make the best use of their natural riches and prosper. Other societies are not so fortunate, and despite their best efforts, may attain only a meager level of well-being because of resource scarcities.[48] Beitz views the resource redistribution principle as giving each society a fair chance to establish just political institutions and an economy that can fulfill its members' basic needs. Affirming this principle "provides assurance to persons in resource-poor societies that their adverse fate will not prevent them from realizing economic conditions sufficient to support just social institutions and to protect human rights."[49] He doesn't explain how the countries with sufficient resources are to redistribute them to resource-poor countries; but no matter.

The global distribution principle that Beitz discusses concerns a situation where production is no longer autarkic and there are flows of trade and services between countries. He believes that in this case a global system of cooperation already exists. In this instance Beitz proposes that a global difference applies (analogous to the principle used in the domestic case in *A Theory of Justice*), giving a principle of distributive justice between societies.[50] Since he believes that the wealthier countries are so because of the greater resources available to them, presumably the global principle (with its scheme of taxation, say) redistributes the benefits of greater resources to resource-poor peoples.

48. Beitz, *Political Theory and International Relations,* p. 137.
49. Ibid., p. 141.
50. Ibid., pp. 153–163.

However, because, as I have said, the crucial element in how a country fares is its political culture—its members' political and civic virtues—and not the level of its resources,[51] the arbitrariness of the distribution of natural resources causes no difficulty. I therefore feel we need not discuss Beitz's resource redistribution principle. On the other hand, if a global principle of distributive justice for the Law of Peoples is meant to apply to our world as it is with its extreme injustices, crippling poverty, and inequalities, its appeal is understandable. But if it is meant to apply continuously without end—without a target, as one might say—in the hypothetical world arrived at after the duty of assistance is fully satisfied, its appeal is questionable. In the latter hypothetical world a global principle gives what we would, I think, regard as unacceptable results. Consider two illustrative cases:

Case (i): two liberal or decent countries are at the same level of wealth (estimated, say, in primary goods) and have the same size population. The first decides to industrialize and to increase its rate of (real) saving, while the second does not. Being content with things as they are, and preferring a more pastoral and leisurely society, the second reaffirms its social values. Some decades later the first country is twice as wealthy as the second. Assuming, as we do, that both societies are liberal or decent, and their peoples free and responsible, and able to make their own decisions, should the industrializing country be taxed to give funds to the second? According to the duty of assistance there would be no tax, and that seems right; whereas with a global egalitarian principle without target, there would always be a flow of taxes as long as the wealth of one people was less than that of the other. This seems unacceptable.

Case (ii) is parallel to (i) except that at the start the rate of population growth in both liberal or decent societies is rather high. Both countries provide the elements of equal justice for women, as required by a well-ordered society; but the first happens to stress these elements, and its women flourish in the political and economic world. As a con-

51. This is powerfully (if sometimes a little too strongly) argued by David Landes in his book *The Wealth and Poverty of Nations* (New York: W. W. Norton, 1998). See his discussion of the OPEC countries, pp. 411–414. Landes thinks that the discovery of oil reserves has been a "monumental misfortune" for the Arab world (p. 414).

sequence, they gradually reach zero population growth that allows for an increasing level of wealth over time. The second society, although it also has these elements of equal justice, because of its prevailing religious and social values, freely held by its women, does not reduce the rate of population growth and it remains rather high.[52] As before, some decades later, the first society is twice as wealthy as the second. Given that both societies are liberal or decent, and their peoples free and responsible, and able to make their own decisions, the duty of assistance does not require taxes from the first, now wealthier society, while the global egalitarian principle without target would. Again, this latter position seems unacceptable.

The crucial point is that the role of the duty of assistance is to assist burdened societies to become full members of the Society of Peoples and to be able to determine the path of their own future for themselves. It is a principle of *transition,* in much the same way that the principle of real saving over time in domestic society is a principle of transition. As explained in §15.2, real saving is meant to lay the foundation for a just basic structure of society, at which point it may cease. In the society of the Law of Peoples the duty of assistance holds until all societies have achieved just liberal or decent basic institutions. Both the duty of real saving and the duty of assistance are defined by a *target* beyond which they no longer hold. They assure the essentials of *political autonomy:* the political autonomy of free and equal citizens in the domestic case, the political autonomy of free and equal liberal and decent peoples in the Society of Peoples.

This raises the question of the difference between a global egalitarian principle and the duty of assistance.[53] That principle is designed

52. Because these basic elements of equal justice for women (including liberty of conscience and freedom of religion) are in place, I assume that the rate of population growth is voluntary, meaning that women are not coerced by their religion or their place in the social structure. This obviously calls for more discussion than I can give here.

53. For a statement of Pogge's own view see his "Human Flourishing and Universal Justice," to appear in *Social Philosophy,* 16:1 (1999). Pogge tells me that here his view does have a target and a cutoff point. I mention in the text that this raises the question of how great the difference may be between the duty of assistance and Pogge's global egalitarian view in "Universal Justice." Without the details of his discussion before us, I cannot discuss it further here.

to help the poor all over the world, and it proposes a General Resource Dividend (GRD) on each society to pay into an international fund to be administered for this purpose. The question to ask about it is whether the principle has a target and a cutoff point. The duty of assistance has both: it seeks to raise the world's poor until they are either free and equal citizens of a reasonably liberal society or members of a decent hierarchical society. That is its target. It also has by design a cutoff point, since for each burdened society the principle ceases to apply once the target is reached. A global egalitarian principle could work in a similar way. Call it an egalitarian principle with target. How great is the difference between the duty of assistance and this egalitarian principle? Surely there is a point at which a people's basic needs (estimated in primary goods) are fulfilled and a people can stand on its own. There may be disagreement about when this point comes, but that there is such a point is crucial to the Law of Peoples and its duty of assistance. Depending on how the respective targets and cutoff points are defined, the principles could be much the same, with largely practical matters of taxation and administration to distinguish between them.

16.3. Contrast with Cosmopolitan View. The Law of Peoples assumes that every society has in its population a sufficient array of human capabilities, each in sufficient number so that the society has enough potential human resources to realize just institutions. The final political end of society is to become fully just and stable for the right reasons. Once that end is reached, the Law of Peoples prescribes no further target such as, for example, to raise the standard of living beyond what is necessary to sustain those institutions. Nor is there any justifiable reason for any society's asking for more than is necessary to sustain just institutions, or for further reduction of material inequalities among societies.

These remarks illustrate the contrast between the Law of Peoples and a cosmopolitan view (§11). The ultimate concern of a cosmopolitan view is the well-being of individuals and not the justice of societies. According to that view there is still a question concerning the need for further global distribution, even after each domestic society has achieved internally just institutions. The simplest illustrative case is to suppose that each of two societies satisfies internally the two principles of justice found in *A Theory of Justice*. In these two societies, the worst-off representative person in one is worse off than the worst-off representative person in the other. Suppose it were possible, through some global redistribution that would allow both societies to continue to satisfy the two principles of justice internally, to improve the lot of the worst-off representative person in the first society. Should we prefer the redistribution to the original distribution?

The Law of Peoples is indifferent between the two distributions. The cosmopolitan view, on the other hand, is not indifferent. It is concerned with the well-being of individuals, and hence with whether the well-being of the globally worst-off person can be improved. What is important to the Law of Peoples is the justice and stability for the right reasons of liberal and decent societies, living as members of a Society of well-ordered Peoples.

PART IV

Conclusion

§17. Public Reason and the Law of Peoples

17.1. Law of Peoples not Ethnocentric. In developing the Law of Peoples I said that liberal societies ask how they are to conduct themselves toward other societies from the point of view of their *own* political conceptions. We must always start from where we now are, assuming that we have taken all reasonable precautions to review the grounds of our political conception and to guard against bias and error. To the objection that to proceed thus is ethnocentric or merely western, the reply is: no, not necessarily. Whether it is so turns on the *content* of the Law of Peoples that liberal societies embrace. The objectivity of that law surely depends not on its time, place, or culture of origin, but on whether it satisfies the criterion of reciprocity and belongs to the public reason of the Society of liberal and decent Peoples.

Looking at the Law of Peoples, we see that it does satisfy the criterion of reciprocity (§1.2). It asks of other societies only what they can reasonably grant without submitting to a position of inferiority or domination. Here it is crucial that the Law of Peoples does not require decent societies to abandon or modify their religious institutions and adopt liberal ones. We have supposed that decent societies would affirm the same Law of Peoples that would hold among just liberal societies. This enabled that law to be universal in its reach. It is so because it asks of other societies only what they can reasonably endorse once they are prepared to stand in a relation of fair equality with all other societies. They cannot argue that being in a relation of equality with other peoples is a western idea! In what other relation can a people and its regime reasonably expect to stand?

17.2. Toleration of Decent Peoples. As we have seen, not all peoples can reasonably be required to be liberal. This follows, in fact, from the principle of toleration of a liberal Law of Peoples and its idea of public reason as worked out from a family of liberal conceptions. What conception of toleration of other societies does the Law of Peoples express? And how is it connected with political liberalism? If it should be asked whether liberal societies are, morally speaking, better than decent hierarchical and other decent societies, and therefore whether the world would be a better place if all societies were required to be liberal, those holding a liberal view might think that the answer would be yes. But this answer overlooks the great importance of maintaining mutual respect between peoples and of each people maintaining its self-respect, not lapsing into contempt for the other, on one side, and bitterness and resentment, on the other (see §7.3). These relations are not a matter of the internal (liberal or decent) basic structure of each people viewed separately. Rather, they concern relations of *mutual respect* among peoples, and so constitute an essential part of the basic structure and political climate of the Society of Peoples. For these reasons the Law of Peoples recognizes decent peoples as members of that larger society. With confidence in the ideals of constitutional liberal democratic thought, it respects decent peoples by allowing them to find their own way to honor those ideals.

Comprehensive doctrines play only a restricted role in liberal democratic politics. Questions of constitutional essentials and matters of basic justice are to be settled by a public political conception of justice and its public reason, though all citizens will also look to their comprehensive doctrines. Given the pluralism of liberal democratic societies—a pluralism which is best seen as the outcome of the exercise of human reason under free institutions—affirming such a political conception as a basis of public justification, along with the basic political institutions that realize it, is the most reasonable and deepest basis of social unity available to us.

The Law of Peoples, as I have sketched it, simply extends these same ideas to the political Society of well-ordered Peoples. For that law, which settles fundamental political questions as they arise for the Society of Peoples, must also be based on a public political conception of justice. I have outlined the content of such a political conception and tried to explain how it could be endorsed by well-ordered societies, both liberal and decent. Except as a basis of a *modus vivendi,* expansionist societies of whatever kind could not endorse it. In their case, no peaceful solution exists except domination by one side or the peace of exhaustion.[1]

Some may find this fact hard to accept. That is because it is often thought that the task of philosophy is to uncover a form of argument that will always prove convincing against all other arguments. There is, however, no such argument. Peoples may often have final ends that require them to oppose one another without compromise. And if these ends are regarded as fundamental enough, and if one or more societies should refuse to accept the idea of the politically reasonable and the family of ideas that go with it, an impasse may arise between them, and war comes, as it did between North and South in the American Civil War. Political liberalism begins with terms of the politically reasonable and builds up its case from there. One does not find peace by declaring war irrational or wasteful, though indeed it may be so, but by preparing the way for peoples to develop a basic structure that supports a reasonably just or decent regime and makes possible a reasonable Law of Peoples.

1. In July of 1864, at a low point for the North in the American Civil War, an unofficial peace mission went to Richmond. Jefferson Davis is alleged to have said: "The war . . . must go on until the last man of this generation falls in his tracks . . . unless you acknowledge the right to self-government. We are not fighting for slavery. We are fighting for independence—and that or extermination, we will have." See David Donald, *Lincoln* (New York: Simon and Schuster, 1995), p. 523. In his Annual Message to Congress on December 6, 1864, Lincoln described the situation between North and South as follows: "[Davis] does not attempt to deceive us. He affords us no excuse to deceive ourselves. He cannot voluntarily reaccept the Union; we cannot voluntarily yield it. Between him and us the issue is distinct, simple, and inflexible. It is an issue that can only be tried by war, and decided by victory." Roy F. Basler, ed., *Collected Works of Abraham Lincoln* (New Brunswick: Rutgers University Press, 1953), vol. 8, p. 151.

§18. Reconciliation to Our Social World

18.1. Society of Peoples Is Possible. In §1.1 I said that political philosophy is realistically utopian when it extends what are ordinarily thought of as the limits of practical political possibility. Our hope for the future rests on the belief that the possibilities of our social world allow a reasonably just constitutional democratic society living as a member of a reasonably just Society of Peoples. An essential step to being reconciled to our social world is to see that such a Society of Peoples is indeed possible.

Recall four basic facts to which I have often referred. These facts can be confirmed by reflecting on history and political experience. They were not discovered by social theory; nor should they be in dispute, as they are virtually truisms.

(a) The Fact of Reasonable Pluralism: A basic feature of liberal democracy is the fact of reasonable pluralism—the fact that a plurality of conflicting reasonable comprehensive doctrines, both religious and nonreligious (or secular), is the normal result of the culture of its free institutions. Different and irreconcilable comprehensive doctrines will be united in supporting the idea of equal liberty for all doctrines and the idea of the separation of church and state. Even if each might prefer that the others not exist, the plurality of sects is the greatest assurance each has of its own equal liberty.[2]

(b) The Fact of Democratic Unity in Diversity: This is the fact that in a constitutional democratic society, political and social unity does not require that its citizens be unified by one comprehensive doctrine, religious or nonreligious. Until the end of the seventeenth century, or later, that was not a common view. Religious division was seen as a disaster for a civil polity. It took the experience of actual history to show this view to be false. While it is necessary that there be a public basis of understanding, this is provided in a liberal democratic society by the

---

2. See James Madison: "Where there is such a variety of sects, there cannot be a majority of any one sect to oppress and persecute the rest. . . . The United States abound in such a variety of sects, that it is a strong security against religious persecution." Virginia Convention, June 12, 1788. *Papers of James Madison,* ed. William T. Hutchinson and William M. E. Rachal (Chicago: University of Chicago Press, 1962), vol. 11, p. 130.

reasonableness and rationality of its political and social institutions, the merits of which can be debated in terms of public reason.

(c) The Fact of Public Reason: This is the fact that citizens in a pluralist liberal democratic society realize that they cannot reach agreement, or even approach mutual understanding, on the basis of their irreconcilable comprehensive doctrines. Thus, when citizens are discussing fundamental political questions, they appeal not to those doctrines, but to a reasonable family of political conceptions of right and justice, and so to the idea of the politically reasonable addressed to citizens as citizens. This does not mean that doctrines of faith or nonreligious (secular) doctrines cannot be introduced into political discussion, but rather that citizens introducing them should also provide sufficient grounds in public reason for the political policies that religious or nonreligious doctrines support.[3]

(d) The Fact of Liberal Democratic Peace: This is the fact discussed in §5 that, ideally, well-ordered constitutional democratic societies do not go to war against one another, and they engage in war only in self-defense, or in an alliance defending other liberal or decent peoples. This is principle (5) of the Law of Peoples.[4]

These four facts provide an explanation of why a reasonably just Society of Peoples is possible. I believe that in a society of liberal and decent peoples the Law of Peoples would be honored, if not all the time, then most of the time, so that it would be recognized as governing the relations among them. To show this, one proceeds through the eight principles that would be agreed to (§4.1) and notes that none of them is likely to be violated. Liberal democratic and decent peoples are likely to follow the Law of Peoples among themselves, since that law suits their fundamental interests, and each wishes to honor its agreements with the others and to be known as trustworthy. The principles most likely to be violated are the norms for the just conduct of war against aggressive outlaw states, and the duty of assistance owed to burdened societies. This is because the reasons supporting these principles call

3. See "The Idea of Public Reason Revisited," §4.

4. Montesquieu defines it as "the principle that the various nations should do to one another in times of peace the most good possible, in times of war the least ill possible, without harming their true interests." *The Spirit of Laws,* book 1, chap. 3.

for great foresight and often have powerful passions working against them. But it is the duty of the statesman to convince the public of the enormous importance of these principles.

To see this, recall the discussion of the role of the statesman in the conduct of war against an enemy state, and the emotions and hatreds the statesman must be prepared to resist (§14). Similarly with the duty of assistance: there may be many aspects of the culture and people of a foreign society living under unfavorable conditions that interfere with the natural sympathy of other societies, or that lead them to underestimate, or fail to recognize, the great extent to which human rights are being violated in the foreign society. A sense of social distance and anxiety about the unknown make these feelings stronger. A statesman may find it difficult to convince public opinion in his or her own people of the enormous importance to them of enabling other societies to establish at least decent political and social institutions.

18.2. Limits of Reconciliation. I noted in the Introduction that two ideas motivate the Law of Peoples. The first is that the great evils of human history—unjust war, oppression, religious persecution, slavery, and the rest—result from political injustice, with its cruelties and callousness. The second is that once political injustice has been eliminated by following just (or at least decent) social policies and establishing just (or at least decent) basic institutions, these great evils will eventually disappear. I call a world in which these great evils have been eliminated and just (or at least decent) basic institutions established by both liberal and decent peoples who honor the Law of Peoples a "realistic utopia." This account of realistic utopia shows us, in the tradition of the late writings of Kant, the social conditions under which we can reasonably hope that all liberal and decent peoples may belong, as members in good standing, to a reasonable Society of Peoples.

There are, however, important limits to reconciliation. I mention two. Many persons—call them "fundamentalists" of various religious or secular doctrines which have been historically dominant—could not be reconciled to a social world such as I have described. For them the social world envisaged by political liberalism is a nightmare of social fragmentation and false doctrines, if not positively evil. To be reconciled to a social world, one must be able to see it as both reasonable and rational. Reconciliation requires acknowledging the fact of reasonable pluralism both within liberal and decent societies and in their relations with one another. Moreover, one must also recognize this pluralism as consistent with reasonable comprehensive doctrines, both religious and secular.[5] Yet this last idea is precisely what fundamentalism denies and political liberalism asserts.

A second limitation to reconciliation to a social world that realizes the idea of a realistic utopia is that it may be a social world many of whose members may suffer considerable misfortune and anguish, and may be distraught by spiritual emptiness. (This is the belief of many fundamentalists.) Political liberalism is a liberalism of freedom—in this it stands with Kant, Hegel, and J. S. Mill.[6] It upholds the equal freedom both of liberal and decent peoples and of liberal peoples' free and equal citizens; and it looks to ensure these citizens adequate all-purpose means (primary goods) so that they can make intelligent use of their freedoms. Their spiritual well-being, though, is not guaranteed. Political liberalism does not dismiss spiritual questions as unimportant, but to the contrary, because of their importance, it leaves them for each citizen to decide for himself or herself. This is not to say that religion is somehow "privatized"; instead, it is not "politicized" (that is, perverted and diminished for ideological ends). The division of labor between political and social institutions, on the one hand, and civic society with its many and diverse associations (religious and secular), on the other, is fully maintained.

18.3. Concluding Reflection. The idea of realistic utopia reconciles us to our social world by showing us that a reasonably just constitutional democracy existing as a member of a reasonably just Society of Peoples is *possible.* It establishes that such a world can exist somewhere and at some time, but not that it must be, or will be. Still, one might feel that the possibility of such a liberal and decent political and

---

5. Catholicism since Vatican II, and some forms of Protestantism, Judaism, and Islam are examples of this. See "The Idea of Public Reason Revisited," §3.
6. See §§1.2 and 7.3.

social order is quite irrelevant, so long as this possibility is also not realized.

While realization is, of course, not unimportant, I believe that the very possibility of such a social order can itself reconcile us to the social world. The possibility is not a mere logical possibility, but one that connects with the deep tendencies and inclinations of the social world. For so long as we believe for good reasons that a self-sustaining and reasonably just political and social order both at home and abroad is possible, we can reasonably hope that we or others will someday, somewhere, achieve it; and we can then do something toward this achievement. This alone, quite apart from our success or failure, suffices to banish the dangers of resignation and cynicism. By showing how the social world may realize the features of a realistic utopia, political philosophy provides a long-term goal of political endeavor, and in working toward it gives meaning to what we can do today.

Thus, our answer to the question of whether a reasonably just Society of Peoples is possible affects our attitudes toward the world as a whole. Our answer affects us before we come to actual politics, and limits or inspires how we take part in it. Rejecting the idea of a just and well-ordered Society of Peoples as impossible will affect the quality and tone of those attitudes and will determine our politics in a significant way. In *A Theory of Justice* and *Political Liberalism* I sketched the more reasonable conceptions of justice for a liberal democratic regime and presented a candidate for the most reasonable. In this monograph on the Law of Peoples I have tried to extend these ideas in order to set out the guidelines for a liberal society's foreign policy in a reasonably just Society of Peoples.

If a reasonably just Society of Peoples whose members subordinate their power to reasonable aims is not possible, and human beings are largely amoral, if not incurably cynical and self-centered, one might ask, with Kant, whether it is worthwhile for human beings to live on the earth.[7]

---

7. "If justice perishes, then it is no longer worthwhile for men to live upon the earth." Kant, *Rechtslehre,* in Remark E following §49, Ak:VI:332.

THE IDEA
OF PUBLIC
REASON
REVISITED

The idea of public reason, as I understand it,[1] belongs to a conception of a well-ordered constitutional democratic society. The form and content of this reason—the way it is understood by citizens and how it interprets their political relationship—are part of the idea of democracy itself. This is because a basic feature of democracy is the fact of reasonable pluralism—the fact that a plurality of conflicting reasonable comprehensive doctrines,[2] religious, philosophical, and moral, is the normal result of its culture of free institutions.[3] Citizens realize

1. See *Political Liberalism* (New York: Columbia University Press, paperback edition, 1996), lecture VI, sec. 8.5. References to *Political Liberalism* are given by lecture and section; page numbers are also provided unless the reference refers to an entire lecture, section, or subsection. Note that the 1996 paperback edition of *Political Liberalism* contains a new second introduction which, among other things, tries to make clearer certain aspects of political liberalism. Section 5 of this introduction, on pp. l–lvii, discusses the idea of public reason and sketches several changes I now make in affirming this idea. These are all followed and elaborated in what is presented here and are important to a complete understanding of the argument. Note also that the pagination of the paperback edition is the same as in the original.

2. I shall use the term "doctrine" for comprehensive views of all kinds and the term "conception" for a political conception and its component parts, such as the conception of the person as citizen. The term "idea" is used as a general term and may refer to either as the context determines.

3. Of course, every society also contains numerous unreasonable doctrines. Yet in this essay I am concerned with an ideal normative conception of democratic government, that is, with the conduct of its reasonable citizens and the principles they follow,

that they cannot reach agreement or even approach mutual understanding on the basis of their irreconcilable comprehensive doctrines. In view of this, they need to consider what kinds of reasons they may reasonably give one another when fundamental political questions are at stake. I propose that in public reason comprehensive doctrines of truth or right be replaced by an idea of the politically reasonable addressed to citizens as citizens.[4]

Central to the idea of public reason is that it neither criticizes nor attacks any comprehensive doctrine, religious or nonreligious, except insofar as that doctrine is incompatible with the essentials of public reason and a democratic polity. The basic requirement is that a reasonable doctrine accepts a constitutional democratic regime and its companion idea of legitimate law. While democratic societies will differ in the specific doctrines that are influential and active within them—as they differ in the western democracies of Europe, the United States, Israel, and India—finding a suitable idea of public reason is a concern that faces them all.

§1. The Idea of Public Reason

1.1. The idea of public reason specifies at the deepest level the basic moral and political values that are to determine a constitutional democratic government's relation to its citizens and their relation to one another. In short, it concerns how the political relation is to be understood. Those who reject constitutional democracy with its criterion of reciprocity[5] will of course reject the very idea of public reason. For them the political relation may be that of friend or foe, to those of a particular religious or secular community or those who are not; or it may be a relentless struggle to win the world for the whole truth. Political liberalism does not engage those who think this way. The zeal to

---

assuming them to be dominant and controlling. How far unreasonable doctrines are active and tolerated is to be determined by the principles of justice and the kinds of actions they permit. See §7.2.

4. See §6.2.
5. See §1.2.

embody the whole truth in politics is incompatible with an idea of public reason that belongs with democratic citizenship.

The idea of public reason has a definite structure, and if one or more of its aspects are ignored it can seem implausible, as it does when applied to the background culture.[6] It has five different aspects: (1) the fundamental political questions to which it applies; (2) the persons to whom it applies (government officials and candidates for public office); (3) its content as given by a family of reasonable political conceptions of justice; (4) the application of these conceptions in discussions of coercive norms to be enacted in the form of legitimate law for a democratic people; and (5) citizens' checking that the principles derived from their conceptions of justice satisfy the criterion of reciprocity.

Moreover, such reason is public in three ways: as the reason of free and equal citizens, it is the reason of the public; its subject is the public good concerning questions of fundamental political justice, which questions are of two kinds, constitutional essentials and matters of basic justice;[7] and its nature and content are public, being expressed in public reasoning by a family of reasonable conceptions of political justice reasonably thought to satisfy the criterion of reciprocity.

It is imperative to realize that the idea of public reason does not apply to all political discussions of fundamental questions, but only to discussions of those questions in what I refer to as the public political forum.[8] This forum may be divided into three parts: the discourse of judges in their decisions, and especially of the judges of a supreme court; the discourse of government officials, especially chief executives and legislators; and finally, the discourse of candidates for public office and their campaign managers, especially in their public oratory, party platforms,

6. See the text accompanying notes 12–15.

7. These questions are described in *Political Liberalism,* lecture VI, sec. 5, pp. 227–230. Constitutional essentials concern questions about what political rights and liberties, say, may reasonably be included in a written constitution, when assuming the constitution may be interpreted by a supreme court, or some similar body. Matters of basic justice relate to the basic structure of society and so would concern questions of basic economic and social justice and other things not covered by a constitution.

8. There is no settled meaning of this term. The one I use is not I think peculiar.

and political statements.[9] We need this three-part division because, as I note later, the idea of public reason does not apply in the same way in these three cases and elsewhere.[10] In discussing what I call the wide view of public political culture,[11] we shall see that the idea of public reason applies more strictly to judges than to others, but that the requirements of public justification for that reason are always the same.

Distinct and separate from this three-part public political forum is what I call the background culture.[12] This is the culture of civil society. In a democracy, this culture is not, of course, guided by any one central idea or principle, whether political or religious. Its many and diverse agencies and associations with their internal life reside within a framework of law that ensures the familiar liberties of thought and speech, and the right of free association.[13] The idea of public reason does not apply to the background culture with its many forms of nonpublic reason nor to media of any kind.[14] Sometimes those who appear to reject the idea of public reason actually mean to assert the need for full and open discussion in the background culture.[15] With this political liberalism fully agrees.

9. Here we face the question of where to draw the line between candidates and those who manage their campaigns and other politically engaged citizens generally. We settle this matter by making candidates and those who run their campaigns responsible for what is said and done on the candidates' behalf.

10. Often writers on this topic use terms that do not distinguish the parts of public discussion, for example, such terms as "the public square," "the public forum," and the like. I follow Kent Greenawalt in thinking a finer division is necessary. See Kent Greenawalt, *Religious Convictions and Political Choice* (Oxford: Oxford University Press, 1988), pp. 226–227 (describing, for example, the differences between a religious leader's preaching or promoting a pro-life organization and leading a major political movement or running for political office).

11. See §4.

12. See *Political Liberalism,* lecture I, sec. 2.3, p. 14.

13. The background culture includes, then, the culture of churches and associations of all kinds, and institutions of learning at all levels, especially universities and professional schools, scientific and other societies. In addition, the nonpublic political culture mediates between the public political culture and the background culture. This comprises media—properly so-named—of all kinds: newspapers, reviews and magazines, television and radio, and much else. Compare these divisions with Habermas's account of the public sphere. See *Political Liberalism,* lecture IX, sec. 1.3, p. 382 n. 13.

14. See ibid., lecture VI, sec. 3, pp. 220–222.

15. See David Hollenbach, S.J., "Civil Society: Beyond the Public-Private Dichotomy," *The Responsive Community,* 5 (Winter 1994–1995): 15. For example, he says:

Finally, distinct from the idea of public reason, as set out by the five features above, is the *ideal* of public reason. This ideal is realized, or satisfied, whenever judges, legislators, chief executives, and other government officials, as well as candidates for public office, act from and follow the idea of public reason and explain to other citizens their reasons for supporting fundamental political positions in terms of the political conception of justice they regard as the most reasonable. In this way they fulfill what I shall call their duty of civility to one another and to other citizens. Hence, whether judges, legislators, and chief executives act from and follow public reason is continually shown in their speech and conduct on a daily basis.

How though is the ideal of public reason realized by citizens who are not government officials? In a representative government citizens vote for representatives—chief executives, legislators, and the like—and not for particular laws (except at a state or local level when they may vote directly on referenda questions, which are rarely fundamental questions). To answer this question, we say that ideally citizens are to think of themselves *as if* they were legislators and ask themselves what statutes, supported by what reasons satisfying the criterion of reciprocity, they would think it most reasonable to enact.[16] When firm and widespread, the disposition of citizens to view themselves as ideal legislators, and to repudiate government officials and candidates for public office who violate public reason, is one of the political and so-

---

"Conversation and argument about the common good will not occur initially in the legislature or in the political sphere (narrowly conceived as the domain in which interests and power are adjudicated). Rather it will develop freely in those components of civil society that are the primary bearers of cultural meaning and value—universities, religious communities, the world of arts, and serious journalism. It can occur wherever thoughtful men and women bring their beliefs on the meaning of the good life into intelligent and critical encounter with understandings of this good held by other peoples with other traditions. In short, it occurs wherever education about and serious inquiry into the meaning of the good life takes place" (ibid., p. 22).

16. There is some resemblance between this criterion and Kant's principle of the original contract. See Immanuel Kant, *The Metaphysics of Morals: Metaphysical First Principles of the Doctrine of Right*, secs. 47–49 (Ak. 6:315–318), ed. and trans. Mary Gregor (Cambridge: Cambridge University Press, 1996), pp. 92–95; Immanuel Kant, *On the Common Saying: "This May be True in Theory, but it does not Apply in Practice,"* pt. II (Ak. VIII:289–306), in *Kant: Political Writings*, ed. Hans Reiss, trans. H. B. Nisbet (Cambridge: Cambridge University Press, 2d ed., 1991), pp. 73–87.

cial roots of democracy, and is vital to its enduring strength and vigor.[17] Thus citizens fulfill their duty of civility and support the idea of public reason by doing what they can to hold government officials to it. This duty, like other political rights and duties, is an intrinsically moral duty. I emphasize that it is not a legal duty, for in that case it would be incompatible with freedom of speech.

1.2. I now turn to a discussion of what I have labeled the third, fourth, and fifth aspects of public reason. The idea of public reason arises from a conception of democratic citizenship in a constitutional democracy. This fundamental political relation of citizenship has two special features: first, it is a relation of citizens within the basic structure of society, a structure we enter only by birth and exit only by death;[18] and second, it is a relation of free and equal citizens who exercise ultimate political power as a collective body. These two features immediately give rise to the question of how, when constitutional essentials and matters of basic justice are at stake, citizens so related can be bound to honor the structure of their constitutional democratic regime and abide by the statutes and laws enacted under it. The fact of reasonable pluralism raises this question all the more sharply, since it means that the differences between citizens arising from their comprehensive doctrines, religious and nonreligious, may be irreconcilable. By what ideals and principles, then, are citizens who share equally in ultimate political power to exercise that power so that each can reasonably justify his or her political decisions to everyone?

To answer this question we say: Citizens are reasonable when, viewing one another as free and equal in a system of social cooperation over generations, they are prepared to offer one another fair terms of cooperation according to what they consider the most reasonable conception of political justice; and when they agree to act on those terms, even at the cost of their own interests in particular situations, provided that other citizens also accept those terms. The criterion of reciprocity requires that when those terms are proposed as the most reasonable terms of fair cooperation, those proposing them must also think it at

17. See also §4.2.
18. See *Political Liberalism,* lecture I, sec. 2.1, p. 12. For concerns about exiting only by death, see ibid., lecture IV, sec. 1.2, p. 136 n. 4.

least reasonable for others to accept them, as free and equal citizens, and not as dominated or manipulated, or under the pressure of an inferior political or social position.[19] Citizens will of course differ as to which conceptions of political justice they think the most reasonable, but they will agree that all are reasonable, even if barely so.

Thus when, on a constitutional essential or matter of basic justice, all appropriate government officials act from and follow public reason, and when all reasonable citizens think of themselves ideally as if they were legislators following public reason, the legal enactment expressing the opinion of the majority is legitimate law. It may not be thought the most reasonable, or the most appropriate, by each, but it is politically (morally) binding on him or her as a citizen and is to be accepted as such. Each thinks that all have spoken and voted at least reasonably, and therefore all have followed public reason and honored their duty of civility.

Hence the idea of political legitimacy based on the criterion of reciprocity says: Our exercise of political power is proper only when we sincerely believe that the reasons we would offer for our political actions—were we to state them as government officials—are sufficient, and we also reasonably think that other citizens might also reasonably accept those reasons. This criterion applies on two levels: one is to the constitutional structure itself, the other is to particular statutes and laws enacted in accordance with that structure. To be reasonable, political conceptions must justify only constitutions that satisfy this principle.

To make more explicit the role of the criterion of reciprocity as expressed in public reason, note that its role is to specify the nature of the political relation in a constitutional democratic regime as one of civic friendship. For this criterion, when government officers act from it in their public reasoning and other citizens support it, shapes the form of their fundamental institutions. For example—I cite an easy case—if we

---

19. The idea of reciprocity has an important place in Amy Gutmann and Dennis Thompson, *Democracy and Disagreement* (Cambridge, Mass.: Harvard University Press, 1996), chaps. 1–2 and passim. However, the meaning and setting of our views are not the same. Public reason in political liberalism is purely political, although political values are intrinsically moral, whereas Gutmann and Thompson's account is more general and seems to work from a comprehensive doctrine.

argue that the religious liberty of some citizens is to be denied, we must give them reasons they can not only understand—as Servetus could understand why Calvin wanted to burn him at the stake—but reasons we might reasonably expect that they, as free and equal citizens, might reasonably also accept. The criterion of reciprocity is normally violated whenever basic liberties are denied. For what reasons can both satisfy the criterion of reciprocity and justify denying to some persons religious liberty, holding others as slaves, imposing a property qualification on the right to vote, or denying the right of suffrage to women?

Since the idea of public reason specifies at the deepest level the basic political values and specifies how the political relation is to be understood, those who believe that fundamental political questions should be decided by what they regard as the best reasons according to their own idea of the whole truth—including their religious or secular comprehensive doctrine—and not by reasons that might be shared by all citizens as free and equal, will of course reject the idea of public reason. Political liberalism views this insistence on the whole truth in politics as incompatible with democratic citizenship and the idea of legitimate law.

1.3. Democracy has a long history, from its beginning in classical Greece down to the present day, and there are many different ideas of democracy.[20] Here I am concerned only with a well-ordered constitutional democracy—a term I used at the outset—understood also as a deliberative democracy. The definitive idea for deliberative democracy is the idea of deliberation itself. When citizens deliberate, they exchange views and debate their supporting reasons concerning public political questions. They suppose that their political opinions may be revised by discussion with other citizens; and therefore these opinions are not simply a fixed outcome of their existing private or nonpoliti-

20. For a useful historical survey see David Held, *Models of Democracy,* 2d ed. (Stanford: Stanford University Press, 1997). Held's numerous models cover the period from the ancient polis to the present time, and he concludes by asking what democracy should mean today. In between he considers the several forms of classical republicanism and classical liberalism, as well as Schumpeter's conception of competitive elite democracy. Some figures discussed include Plato and Aristotle; Marsilius of Padua and Machiavelli; Hobbes and Madison; Bentham, James Mill, and John Stuart Mill; Marx with socialism and communism. These are paired with schematized models of the characteristic institutions and their roles.

cal interests. It is at this point that public reason is crucial, for it characterizes such citizens' reasoning concerning constitutional essentials and matters of basic justice. While I cannot fully discuss the nature of deliberative democracy here, I note a few key points to indicate the wider place and role of public reason.

There are three essential elements of deliberative democracy. One is an idea of public reason,[21] although not all such ideas are the same. A second is a framework of constitutional democratic institutions that specifies the setting for deliberative legislative bodies. The third is the knowledge and desire on the part of citizens generally to follow public reason and to realize its ideal in their political conduct. Immediate implications of these essentials are the public financing of elections, and the providing for public occasions of orderly and serious discussion of fundamental questions and issues of public polity. Public deliberation must be made possible, recognized as a basic feature of democracy, and set free from the curse of money.[22] Otherwise politics is dominated by corporate and other organized interests who through large contributions to campaigns distort if not preclude public discussion and deliberation.

Deliberative democracy also recognizes that without widespread education in the basic aspects of constitutional democratic government for all citizens, and without a public informed about pressing problems, crucial political and social decisions simply cannot be made. Even

21. Deliberative democracy limits the reasons citizens may give in supporting their political opinions to reasons consistent with their seeing other citizens as equals. See Joshua Cohen, "Deliberation and Democratic Legitimacy," in Alan Hamlin and Philip Petit, eds., *The Good Polity: Normative Analysis of the State* (Oxford: Basil Blackwell, 1989), pp. 17, 21, 24; Joshua Cohen, Comment, "Review Symposium on *Democracy and Its Critics*," *Journal of Politics,* 53 (1991): 223–224; Joshua Cohen, "Democracy and Liberty," in Jon Elster, ed., *Deliberative Democracy* (New York: Cambridge University Press, 1998).

22. See Ronald Dworkin, "The Curse of American Politics," *New York Review of Books,* October 17, 1996, p. 19 (describing why "money is the biggest threat to the democratic process"). Dworkin also argues forcefully against the grave error of the Supreme Court in *Buckley v. Valeo,* in *United States Supreme Court Reports,* 424 (1976): 1. Dworkin, *New York Review of Books,* pp. 21–24. See also *Political Liberalism,* lecture VIII, sec. 12, pp. 359–363. (*Buckley* is "dismaying" and raises the risk of "repeating the mistake of the Lochner era.")

should farsighted political leaders wish to make sound changes and reforms, they cannot convince a misinformed and cynical public to accept and follow them. For example, there are sensible proposals for what should be done regarding the alleged coming crisis in Social Security: slow down the growth of benefits levels, gradually raise the retirement age, impose limits on expensive terminal medical care that prolongs life for only a few weeks or days, and finally, raise taxes now, rather than face large increases later.[23] But as things are, those who follow the "great game of politics" know that none of these sensible proposals will be accepted. The same story can be told about the importance of support for international institutions (such as the United Nations), foreign aid properly spent, and concern for human rights at home and abroad. In constant pursuit of money to finance campaigns, the political system is simply unable to function. Its deliberative powers are paralyzed.

§2. The Content of Public Reason

2.1. A citizen engages in public reason, then, when he or she deliberates within a framework of what he or she sincerely regards as the most reasonable political conception of justice, a conception that expresses political values that others, as free and equal citizens might also reasonably be expected reasonably to endorse. Each of us must have principles and guidelines to which we appeal in such a way that this criterion is satisfied. I have proposed that one way to identify those political principles and guidelines is to show that they would be agreed to in what in *Political Liberalism* is called the original position.[24] Others will think that different ways to identify these principles are more reasonable.

Thus, the content of public reason is given by a family of political

---

23. See Paul Krugman, "Demographics and Destiny," *New York Times Book Review*, October 20, 1996, p. 12, reviewing and describing proposals in Peter G. Peterson, *Will America Grow Up Before It Grows Old? How the Coming Social Security Crisis Threatens You, Your Family, and Your Country* (New York: Random House, 1996), and Charles R. Morris, *The AARP: America's Most Powerful Lobby and the Clash of Generations* (New York: Times Books, 1996).

24. *Political Liberalism,* lecture I, sec. 4, pp. 22–28.

conceptions of justice, and not by a single one. There are many liberalisms and related views, and therefore many forms of public reason specified by a family of reasonable political conceptions. Of these, justice as fairness, whatever its merits, is but one. The limiting feature of these forms is the criterion of reciprocity, viewed as applied between free and equal citizens, themselves seen as reasonable and rational. Three main features characterize these conceptions:

First, a list of certain basic rights, liberties, and opportunities
(such as those familiar from constitutional regimes);
Second, an assignment of special priority to those rights, liberties, and opportunities, especially with respect to the claims of the general good and perfectionist values; and
Third, measures ensuring for all citizens adequate all-purpose means to make effective use of their freedoms.[25]

Each of these liberalisms endorses the underlying ideas of citizens as free and equal persons and of society as a fair system of cooperation over time. Yet since these ideas can be interpreted in various ways, we get different formulations of the principles of justice and different contents of public reason. Political conceptions differ also in how they order, or balance, political principles and values even when they specify the same ones. I assume also that these liberalisms contain substantive principles of justice, and hence cover more than procedural justice. They are required to specify the religious liberties and freedoms of artistic expression of equal citizens, as well as substantive ideas of fairness involving fair opportunity and ensuring adequate all-purpose means, and much else.[26]

25. Here I follow the definition in *Political Liberalism,* lecture I, sec. 1.2, p. 6, and lecture IV, sec. 5.3, pp. 156–157.

26. Some may think the fact of reasonable pluralism means that the only forms of fair adjudication between comprehensive doctrines must be only procedural and not substantive. This view is forcefully argued by Stuart Hampshire in *Innocence and Experience* (Cambridge, Mass.: Harvard University Press, 1989). In the text above, however, I assume the several forms of liberalism are each substantive conceptions. For a thorough treatment of these issues, see the discussion in Joshua Cohen, "Pluralism and Proceduralism," *Chicago-Kent Law Review,* 69, no. 3 (1994): 589–618.

Political liberalism, then, does not try to fix public reason once and for all in the form of one favored political conception of justice.[27] That would not be a sensible approach. For instance, political liberalism also admits Habermas's discourse conception of legitimacy (sometimes said to be radically democratic rather than liberal),[28] as well as Catholic views of the common good and solidarity when they are expressed in terms of political values.[29] Even if relatively few conceptions come to dominate over time, and one conception even appears to have a special central place, the forms of permissible public reason are always several. Moreover, new variations may be proposed from time to time and older ones may cease to be represented. It is important that this be so; otherwise the claims of groups or interests

27. I do think that justice as fairness has a certain special place in the family of political conceptions, as I suggest in *Political Liberalism,* lecture IV, sec. 7.4. But this opinion of mine is not basic to the ideas of political liberalism and public reason.

28. See Jürgen Habermas, *Between Facts and Norms: Contributions to a Discourse Theory of Law and Democracy,* trans. William Rehg (Cambridge, Mass.: MIT Press, 1996), pp. 107–109. Seyla Benhabib in her discussion of models of public space in *Situating the Self: Gender, Community, and Postmodernism in Contemporary Ethics* (London: Routledge, 1992) says that "the discourse model is the only one which is compatible both with the general social trends of our societies and with the emancipatory aspirations of new social movements like the women's movement" (p. 113). She has previously considered Arendt's agonistic conception, as Benhabib calls it, and that of political liberalism. But I find it hard to distinguish her view from that of a form of political liberalism and public reason, since it turns out that she means by the public sphere what Habermas does, namely what *Political Liberalism* calls the background culture of civil society in which the ideal of public reason does not apply. Hence political liberalism is not limiting in the way she thinks. Also, Benhabib does not try to show, so far as I can see, that certain principles of right and justice belonging to the content of public reason could not be interpreted to deal with the problems raised by the women's movement. I doubt that this can be done. The same holds for Benhabib's earlier remarks in Seyla Benhabib, "Liberal Dialogue versus a Critical Theory of Discursive Legitimation," in *Liberalism and the Moral Life,* ed. Nancy Rosenblum (Cambridge, Mass.: Harvard University Press, 1989), pp. 143, 154–156, in which the problems of the women's movement were discussed in a similar way.

29. Deriving from Aristotle and St. Thomas, the idea of the common good is essential to much of Catholic moral and political thought. See, for example, John Finnis, *Natural Law and Natural Rights* (Oxford: Clarendon Press, 1980), pp. 153–156, 160; Jacques Maritain, *Man and the State* (Chicago: University of Chicago Press, 1951), pp. 108–114. Finnis is especially clear, while Aquinas is occasionally ambiguous.

arising from social change might be repressed and fail to gain their appropriate political voice.[30]

2.2. We must distinguish public reason from what is sometimes referred to as secular reason and secular values. These are not the same as public reason. For I define secular reason as reasoning in terms of comprehensive nonreligious doctrines. Such doctrines and values are much too broad to serve the purposes of public reason. Political values are not moral doctrines,[31] however available or accessible these may be to our reason and common sense reflection. Moral doctrines are on a level with religion and first philosophy. By contrast, liberal political principles and values, although intrinsically moral values, are specified by liberal political conceptions of justice and fall under the category of the political. These political conceptions have three features:

First, their principles apply to basic political and social institutions (the basic structure of society);
Second, they can be presented independently from comprehensive doctrines of any kind (although they may, of course, be supported by a reasonable overlapping consensus of such doctrines); and
Finally, they can be worked out from fundamental ideas seen as implicit in the public political culture of a constitutional regime, such as the conceptions of citizens as free and equal persons, and of society as a fair system of cooperation.

Thus, the content of public reason is given by the principles and values of the family of liberal political conceptions of justice meeting these conditions. To engage in public reason is to appeal to one of these polit-

---

30. Thus, Jeremy Waldron's criticism of political liberalism as not allowing new and changing conceptions of political justice is incorrect. See Jeremy Waldron, "Religious Contributions in Public Deliberation," *San Diego Law Review,* 30 (1993): 837–838. See the reply to Waldron's criticisms in Lawrence B. Solum, "Novel Public Reasons," *Loyola LA Law Review,* 29 (1996): 1460. ("General acceptance of a liberal ideal of public reason would permit the robust evolution of political discourse.")

31. See note 2 for my definition of "doctrine."

ical conceptions—to their ideals and principles, standards and values—when debating fundamental political questions. This requirement still allows us to introduce into political discussion at any time our comprehensive doctrine, religious or nonreligious, provided that, in due course, we give properly public reasons to support the principles and policies our comprehensive doctrine is said to support. I refer to this requirement as *the proviso,* and consider it in detail below.[32]

A feature of public reasoning, then, is that it proceeds entirely within a political conception of justice. Examples of political values include those mentioned in the preamble to the United States Constitution: a more perfect union, justice, domestic tranquillity, the common defense, the general welfare, and the blessings of liberty for ourselves and our posterity. These include under them other values: so, for example, under justice we also have equal basic liberties, equality of opportunity, ideals concerning the distribution of income and taxation, and much else.

The political values of public reason are distinct from other values in that they are realized in and characterize political institutions. This does not mean that analogous values cannot characterize other social forms. The values of effectiveness and efficiency may characterize the social organization of teams and clubs, as well as the political institutions of the basic structure of society. But a value is properly political only when the social form is itself political: when it is realized, say, in parts of the basic structure and its political and social institutions. It follows that many political conceptions are nonliberal, including those of aristocracy and corporate oligarchy, and of autocracy and dictatorship. All of these fall within the category of the political.[33] We, however, are concerned only with those political conceptions that are reasonable for a constitutional democratic regime, and as the preceding paragraphs make clear, these are the ideals and principles expressed by reasonable liberal political conceptions.

2.3. Another essential feature of public reason is that its political conceptions should be complete. This means that each conception

---

32. See §4.
33. Here see *Political Liberalism,* lecture IX, sec. 1.1, pp. 374–375.

should express principles, standards, and ideals, along with guidelines of inquiry, such that the values specified by it can be suitably ordered or otherwise united so that those values alone give a reasonable answer to all, or to nearly all, questions involving constitutional essentials and matters of basic justice. Here the ordering of values is made in the light of their structure and features within the political conception itself, and not primarily from how they occur within citizens' comprehensive doctrines. Political values are not to be ordered by viewing them separately and detached from one another or from any definite context. They are not puppets manipulated from behind the scenes by comprehensive doctrines.[34] The ordering is not distorted by those doctrines provided that public reason sees the ordering as reasonable. And public reason can indeed see an ordering of political values as reasonable (or unreasonable), since institutional structures are open to view and mistakes and gaps within the political ordering will become exposed. Thus, we may be confident that the ordering of political values is not distorted by particular reasonable comprehensive doctrines. (I emphasize that the only criterion of distortion is that the ordering of political values be itself unreasonable.)

The significance of completeness lies in the fact that unless a political conception is complete, it is not an adequate framework of thought in the light of which the discussion of fundamental political questions can be carried out.[35] What we cannot do in public reason is

34. This thought I owe to Peter de Marneffe.

35. Note here that different political conceptions of justice will represent different interpretations of the constitutional essentials and matters of basic justice. There are also different interpretations of the same conception, since its concepts and values may be taken in different ways. There is not, then, a sharp line between where a political conception ends and its interpretation begins, nor need there be. All the same, a conception greatly limits its possible interpretations; otherwise discussion and argument could not proceed. For example, a constitution declaring the freedom of religion, including the freedom to affirm no religion, along with the separation of church and state, may appear to leave open the question whether church schools may receive public funds, and if so, in what way. The difference here might be seen as how to interpret the same political conception, one interpretation allowing public funds, the other not; or alternatively, as the difference between two political conceptions. In the absence of particulars, it does not matter which we call it. The important point is that since the content of public reason is a family of political conceptions, that content admits the interpretations we may need. It is not as if we were stuck with a fixed conception, much

to proceed directly from our comprehensive doctrine, or a part thereof, to one or several political principles and values, and the particular institutions they support. Instead, we are required first to work to the basic ideas of a complete political conception and from there to elaborate its principles and ideals, and to use the arguments they provide. Otherwise public reason allows arguments that are too immediate and fragmentary.

2.4. I now note several examples of political principles and values to illustrate the more specific content of public reason, and particularly the various ways in which the criterion of reciprocity is both applicable and subject to violation.

(a) As a first example, consider the value of autonomy. It may take two forms: one is political autonomy, the legal independence and assured integrity of citizens and their sharing equally with others in the exercise of political power; the other is purely moral and characterizes a certain way of life and reflection, critically examining our deepest ends and ideals, as in Mill's ideal of individuality.[36] Whatever we may think of autonomy as a purely moral value, it fails to satisfy, given reasonable pluralism, the constraint of reciprocity, as many citizens, for example, those holding certain religious doctrines, may reject it. Thus moral autonomy is not a political value, whereas political autonomy is.

(b) As a second example, consider the familiar story of the Good Samaritan. Are the values appealed to properly political values and not simply religious or philosophical values? While the wide view of public political culture allows us, in making a proposal, to introduce the Gospel story, public reason requires us to justify our proposal in terms of proper political values.[37]

---

less with one interpretation of it. This is a comment on Kent Greenawalt, *Private Consciences and Public Reasons* (Oxford: Oxford University Press, 1995), pp. 113–120, where *Political Liberalism* is said to have difficulty dealing with the problem of determining the interpretation of political conceptions.

36. John Stuart Mill, *On Liberty* (1859), chap. 3, paras. 1–9, in *Collected Works of John Stuart Mill*, ed. John M. Robson (Toronto: University of Toronto Press, 1977), vol. 18, pp. 260–275.

37. See §4.1 on the proviso and the example of citing the Gospel story. For a detailed consideration of the wide view of public political culture, see generally §4.

(c) As a third example, consider appeals to desert in discussing the fair distribution of income: people are wont to say that ideally distribution should be in accordance with desert. What sense of desert do they have in mind? Do they mean that persons in various offices should have the requisite qualifications—judges must be qualified to judge—and all should have a fair opportunity to qualify themselves for favored positions? That is indeed a political value. But distribution in accordance with moral desert, where this means the moral worth of character, all things considered, and including comprehensive doctrines, is not. It is not a feasible political and social aim.

(d) Finally, consider the state's interest in the family and human life. How should the political value invoked be specified correctly? Traditionally it has been specified very broadly. But in a democratic regime the government's legitimate interest is that public law and policy should support and regulate, in an ordered way, the institutions needed to reproduce political society over time. These include the family (in a form that is just), arrangements for rearing and educating children, and institutions of public health generally. This ordered support and regulation rest on political principles and values, since political society is regarded as existing in perpetuity and so as maintaining itself and its institutions and culture over generations. Given this interest, the government would appear to have no interest in the particular form of family life, or of relations among the sexes, except insofar as that form or those relations in some way affect the orderly reproduction of society over time. Thus, appeals to monogamy as such, or against same-sex marriages, as within the government's legitimate interest in the family, would reflect religious or comprehensive moral doctrines. Accordingly, that interest would appear improperly specified. Of course, there may be other political values in the light of which such a specification would pass muster: for example, if monogamy were necessary for the equality of women, or same-sex marriages destructive to the raising and educating of children.[38]

2.5. The four examples bring out a contrast to what I have above

---

38. Of course, I don't attempt to decide the question here, since we are concerned only with the kinds of reasons and considerations that public reasoning involves.

called secular reason.[39] A view often expressed is that while religious reasons and sectarian doctrines should not be invoked to justify legislation in a democratic society, sound secular arguments may be.[40] But what is a secular argument? Some think of any argument that is reflective and critical, publicly intelligible and rational, as a secular argument; and they discuss various such arguments for considering, say, homosexual relations unworthy or degrading.[41] Of course, some of these arguments may be reflective and rational secular ones (as so defined). Nevertheless, a central feature of political liberalism is that it views all such arguments the same way it views religious ones, and therefore these secular philosophical doctrines do not provide public reasons. Secular concepts and reasoning of this kind belong to first philosophy and moral doctrine, and fall outside of the domain of the political.

Thus, in considering whether to make homosexual relations between citizens criminal offenses, the question is not whether those relations are precluded by a worthy idea of full human good as characterized by a sound philosophical and nonreligious view, nor whether those of religious faith regard it as sin, but primarily whether legislative statutes forbidding those relations infringe the civil rights of free and equal democratic citizens.[42] This question calls for a reasonable political conception of justice specifying those civil rights, which are always a matter of constitutional essentials.

39. See §2.2.

40. See Robert Audi, "The Place of Religious Argument in a Free and Democratic Society," *San Diego Law Review,* 30 (1993): 677. Here Audi defines a secular reason as follows: "A secular reason is roughly one whose normative force does not evidentially depend on the existence of God or on theological considerations, or on the pronouncements of a person or institution qua religious authority" (p. 692). This definition is ambiguous between secular reasons in the sense of a nonreligious comprehensive doctrine and in the sense of a purely political conception within the content of public reason. Depending on which is meant, Audi's view that secular reasons must also be given along with religious reasons might have a role similar to what I call the proviso in §4.1.

41. See the discussion by Michael Perry of John Finnis's argument, which denies that such relations are compatible with human good. *Religion in Politics: Constitutional and Moral Perspectives* (Oxford: Oxford University Press, 1997), chap. 3, pp. 85–86.

42. Here I follow T. M. Scanlon's view in "The Difficulty of Tolerance," in *Toleration: An Elusive Virtue,* ed. David Heyd (Princeton: Princeton University Press, 1996), pp. 226–239. While the whole is instructive, sec. 3, pp. 230–233, is especially relevant here.

§3. Religion and Public Reason in Democracy

3.1. Before examining the idea of the wide view of public political culture, we ask: How is it possible for those holding religious doctrines, some based on religious authority, for example, the Church or the Bible, to hold at the same time a reasonable political conception that supports a reasonable constitutional democratic regime? Can these doctrines still be compatible for the right reasons with a liberal political conception? To attain this compatibility, it is not sufficient that these doctrines accept a democratic government merely as a *modus vivendi*. Referring to citizens holding religious doctrines as citizens of faith, we ask: How is it possible for citizens of faith to be wholehearted members of a democratic society who endorse society's intrinsic political ideals and values and do not simply acquiesce in the balance of political and social forces? Expressed more sharply: How is it possible— or is it—for those of faith, as well as the nonreligious (secular), to endorse a constitutional regime even when their comprehensive doctrines may not prosper under it, and indeed may decline? This last question brings out anew the significance of the idea of legitimacy and public reason's role in determining legitimate law.

To clarify the question, consider two examples. The first is that of Catholics and Protestants in the sixteenth and seventeenth centuries when the principle of toleration was honored only as a *modus vivendi*.[43] This meant that should either party fully gain its way it would impose its own religious doctrine as the sole admissible faith. A society in which many faiths all share this attitude and assume that for the indefinite future their relative numbers will stay roughly the same might well have a constitution resembling that of the United States, fully protecting the religious liberties of sharply divided religions more or less equal in political power. The constitution is, as it were, honored as a pact to maintain civil peace.[44] In this society political issues might be discussed in terms of political ideas and values so as not to open religious conflict and arouse sectarian hostility. The role of public reason

43. See *Political Liberalism,* lecture IV, sec. 3.4, p. 148.
44. See Kent Greenawalt's example of the society of Diverse Fervent Believers in Greenawalt, *Private Consciences and Public Reasons,* pp. 16–18, 21–22.

here serves merely to quiet divisiveness and encourage social stability. However, in this case we do not have stability for the right reasons, that is, as secured by a firm allegiance to a democratic society's political (moral) ideals and values.

Nor again do we have stability for the right reasons in the second example—a democratic society where citizens accept as political (moral) principles the substantive constitutional clauses that ensure religious, political, and civil liberties, when their allegiance to these constitutional principles is so limited that none is willing to see his or her religious or nonreligious doctrine losing ground in influence and numbers, and such citizens are prepared to resist or to disobey laws that they think undermine their positions. And they do this even though the full range of religious and other liberties is always maintained and the doctrine in question is completely secure. Here again democracy is accepted conditionally and not for the right reasons.

What these examples have in common is that society is divided into separate groups, each of which has its own fundamental interest distinct from and opposed to the interests of the other groups and for which it is prepared to resist or to violate legitimate democratic law. In the first example, it is the interest of a religion in establishing its hegemony, while in the second, it is the doctrine's fundamental interest in maintaining a certain degree of success and influence for its own view, either religious or nonreligious. While a constitutional regime can fully ensure rights and liberties for all permissible doctrines, and therefore protect our freedom and security, a democracy necessarily requires that, as one equal citizen among others, each of us accept the obligations of legitimate law.[45] While no one is expected to put his or her religious or nonreligious doctrine in danger, we must each give up forever the hope of changing the constitution so as to establish our religion's hegemony, or of qualifying our obligations so as to ensure its influence and success. To retain such hopes and aims would be inconsistent with the idea of equal basic liberties for all free and equal citizens.

3.2. To expand on what we asked earlier: How is it possible—or is

45. See *Political Liberalism,* lecture V, sec. 6, pp. 195–200.

it—for those of faith, as well as the nonreligious (secular), to endorse a constitutional regime even when their comprehensive doctrines may not prosper under it, and indeed may decline? Here the answer lies in the religious or nonreligious doctrine's understanding and accepting that, except by endorsing a reasonable constitutional democracy, there is no other way fairly to ensure the liberty of its adherents consistent with the equal liberties of other reasonable free and equal citizens. In endorsing a constitutional democratic regime, a religious doctrine may say that such are the limits God sets to our liberty; a nonreligious doctrine will express itself otherwise.[46] But in either case, these doctrines formulate in different ways how liberty of conscience and the principle of toleration can cohere with equal justice for all citizens in a reasonable democratic society. Thus, the principles of toleration and lib-

46. An example of how a religion may do this is the following. Abdullahi Ahmed An-Na'im, in his book *Toward an Islamic Reformation: Civil Liberties, Human Rights, and International Law* (Syracuse: Syracuse University Press, 1990), pp. 52–57, introduces the idea of reconsidering the traditional interpretation of Shari'a, which for Muslims is divine law. For his interpretation to be accepted by Muslims, it must be presented as the correct and superior interpretation of Shari'a. The basic idea of An-Na'im's interpretation, following the late Sudanese author *Ustadh* Mahmoud Mohamed Taha, is that the traditional understanding of Shari'a has been based on the teachings of the later Medina period of Muhammad, whereas the teachings of the earlier Mecca period of Muhammad are the eternal and fundamental message of Islam. An-Na'im claims that the superior Mecca teachings and principles were rejected in favor of the more realistic and practical (in a seventh-century historical context) Medina teachings because society was not yet ready for their implementation. Now that historical conditions have changed, An-Na'im believes that Muslims should follow the earlier Mecca period in interpreting Shari'a. So interpreted, he says that Shari'a supports constitutional democracy (ibid., pp. 69–100).

In particular, the earlier Mecca interpretation of Shari'a supports equality of men and women, and complete freedom of choice in matters of faith and religion, both of which are in accordance with the constitutional principle of equality before the law. An-Na'im writes: "The Qur'an does not mention constitutionalism, but human rational thinking and experience have shown that constitutionalism is necessary for realizing the just and good society prescribed by the Qur'an. An Islamic justification and support for constitutionalism is important and relevant for Muslims. Non-Muslims may have their own secular or other justifications. As long as all are agreed on the principle and specific rules of constitutionalism, including complete equality and non-discrimination on grounds of gender or religion, each may have his or her own reasons for coming to that agreement" (ibid., p. 100). (This is a perfect example of overlapping consensus.) I thank Akeel Bilgrami for informing me of An-Na'im's work. I also owe thanks to Roy Mottahedeh for valuable discussion.

erty of conscience must have an essential place in any constitutional democratic conception. They lay down the fundamental basis to be accepted by all citizens as fair and regulative of the rivalry between doctrines.

Observe here that there are two ideas of toleration. One is purely political, being expressed in terms of the rights and duties protecting religious liberty in accordance with a reasonable political conception of justice. The other is not purely political but expressed from within a religious or a nonreligious doctrine, as when, for example, it was said above that such are the limits God sets on our liberty. Saying this offers an example of what I call reasoning from conjecture.[47] In this case we reason from what we believe, or conjecture, may be other people's basic doctrines, religious or philosophical, and seek to show them that, despite what they might think, they can still endorse a reasonable political conception of justice. We are not ourselves asserting that ground of toleration but offering it as one they could assert consistent with their comprehensive doctrines.

§4. The Wide View of Public Political Culture

4.1. Now we consider what I call the wide view of public political culture and discuss two aspects of it. The first is that reasonable comprehensive doctrines, religious or nonreligious, may be introduced in public political discussion at any time, provided that in due course proper political reasons—and not reasons given solely by comprehensive doctrines—are presented that are sufficient to support whatever the comprehensive doctrines introduced are said to support. This injunction to present proper political reasons I refer to as *the proviso,* and it specifies public political culture as distinct from the background culture.[48] The second aspect I consider is that there may be positive reasons for introducing comprehensive doctrines into public political discussion. I take up these two aspects in turn.

47. See §4.3.
48. See *Political Liberalism,* lecture I, sec. 2.3, pp. 13–14 (contrasting public political culture with background culture).

Obviously, many questions may be raised about how to satisfy the proviso.[49] One is: when does it need to be satisfied? On the same day or some later day? Also, on whom does the obligation to honor it fall? It is important that it be clear and established that the proviso is to be appropriately satisfied in good faith. Yet the details about how to satisfy this proviso must be worked out in practice and cannot feasibly be governed by a clear family of rules given in advance. How they work out is determined by the nature of the public political culture and calls for good sense and understanding. It is important also to observe that the introduction into public political culture of religious and secular doctrines, provided the proviso is met, does not change the nature and content of justification in public reason itself. This justification is still given in terms of a family of reasonable political conceptions of justice. However, there are no restrictions or requirements on how religious or secular doctrines are themselves to be expressed; these doctrines need not, for example, be by some standards logically correct, or open to rational appraisal, or evidentially supportable.[50] Whether they are or not is a matter to be decided by those presenting them, and how they want what they say to be taken. They will normally have practical reasons for wanting to make their views acceptable to a broader audience.

4.2. Citizens' mutual knowledge of one another's religious and non-religious doctrines expressed in the wide view of public political culture[51] recognizes that the roots of democratic citizens' allegiance to their political conceptions lie in their respective comprehensive doctrines, both religious and nonreligious. In this way citizens' allegiance to the democratic ideal of public reason is strengthened for the right reasons. We may think of the reasonable comprehensive doctrines that support society's reasonable political conceptions as those conceptions' vital social basis, giving them enduring strength and vigor. When these

49. I am indebted here to valuable discussion with Dennis Thompson.

50. Greenawalt discusses Franklin Gamwell and Michael Perry, who do evidently impose such constraints on how religion is to be presented. See Greenawalt, *Private Consciences and Public Reasons,* pp. 85–95.

51. Again, as always, in distinction from the background culture, where I emphasize there are no restrictions.

doctrines accept the proviso and only then come into political debate, the commitment to constitutional democracy is publicly manifested.[52] Made aware of this commitment, government officials and citizens are more willing to honor the duty of civility, and their following the ideal of public reason helps foster the kind of society that ideal exemplifies. These benefits of the mutual knowledge of citizens' recognizing one another's reasonable comprehensive doctrines bring out a positive ground for introducing such doctrines, which is not merely a defensive ground, as if their intrusion into public discussion were inevitable in any case.

Consider, for example, a highly contested political issue—the issue of public support for church schools.[53] Those on different sides are likely to come to doubt one another's allegiance to basic constitutional and political values. It is wise, then, for all sides to introduce their comprehensive doctrines, whether religious or secular, so as to open the way for them to explain to one another how their views do indeed support those basic political values. Consider also the Abolitionists and those in the Civil Rights Movement.[54] The proviso was fulfilled in their cases,

52. Political liberalism is sometimes criticized for not itself developing accounts of these social roots of democracy and setting out the formation of its religious and other supports. Yet political liberalism does recognize these social roots and stresses their importance. Obviously the political conceptions of toleration and freedom of religion would be impossible in a society in which religious freedom was not honored and cherished. Thus, political liberalism agrees with David Hollenbach, S.J., when he writes: "Not the least important of [the transformations brought about by Aquinas] was his insistence that the political life of a people is not the highest realization of the good of which they are capable—an insight that lies at the root of constitutional theories of limited government. And though the Church resisted the liberal discovery of modern freedoms through much of the modern period, liberalism has been transforming Catholicism once again through the last half of our own century. The memory of these events in social and intellectual history as well as the experience of the Catholic Church since the Second Vatican Council leads me to hope that communities holding different visions of the good life can get somewhere if they are willing to risk conversation and argument about these visions." David Hollenbach, "Contexts of the Political Role of Religion: Civil Society and Culture," *San Diego Law Review,* 30 (1993): 891. While a conception of public reason must recognize the significance of these social roots of constitutional democracy and note how they strengthen its vital institutions, it need not itself undertake a study of these matters. For the need to consider this point, I am indebted to Paul Weithman.

53. See *Political Liberalism,* lecture VI, sec. 8.2, pp. 248–249.

54. See ibid., lecture VI, sec. 8.3, pp. 249–251. I do not know whether the Abolitionists and King thought of themselves as fulfilling the purpose of the proviso. But whether they did or not, they could have. And had they known and accepted the idea of public reason, they would have. I thank Paul Weithman for this point.

however much they emphasized the religious roots of their doctrines, because these doctrines supported basic constitutional values—as they themselves asserted—and so supported reasonable conceptions of political justice.

4.3. Public reasoning aims for public justification. We appeal to political conceptions of justice, and to ascertainable evidence and facts open to public view, in order to reach conclusions about what we think are the most reasonable political institutions and policies. Public justification is not simply valid reasoning, but argument addressed to others: it proceeds correctly from premises we accept and think others could reasonably accept to conclusions we think they could also reasonably accept. This meets the duty of civility, since in due course the proviso is satisfied.

There are two other forms of discourse that may also be mentioned, though neither expresses a form of public reasoning. One is declaration: here we each declare our own comprehensive doctrine, religious or nonreligious. This we do not expect others to share. Rather, each of us shows how, from our own doctrines, we can and do endorse a reasonable public political conception of justice with its principles and ideals. The aim of doing this is to declare to others who affirm different comprehensive doctrines that we also each endorse a reasonable political conception belonging to the family of reasonable such conceptions. On the wide view, citizens of faith who cite the Gospel parable of the Good Samaritan do not stop there, but go on to give a public justification for this parable's conclusions in terms of political values.[55] In this way citizens who hold different doctrines are reassured, and this strengthens the ties of civic friendship.[56]

The second form is conjecture, defined thus: we argue from what

---

55. Luke 10:29–37. It is easy to see how the Gospel story could be used to support the imperfect moral duty of mutual aid, as found, say, in Kant's fourth example in the *Grundlegung*. See Immanuel Kant, *Groundwork for the Metaphysics of Morals*, Ak. 4:423, in *Practical Philosophy*, trans. Mary Gregor (Cambridge: Cambridge University Press, 1996). To formulate a suitable example in terms of political values only, consider a variant of the difference principle or of some other analogous idea. The principle could be seen as giving a special concern for the poor, as in the Catholic social doctrine. See *A Theory of Justice*, sec. 13 (defining the difference principle).

56. For the relevance of this form of discourse, I am indebted to discussion with Charles Larmore.

we believe, or conjecture, are other people's basic doctrines, religious or secular, and try to show them that, despite what they might think, they can still endorse a reasonable political conception that can provide a basis for public reasons. The ideal of public reason is thereby strengthened. However, it is important that conjecture be sincere and not manipulative. We must openly explain our intentions and state that we do not assert the premises from which we argue, but that we proceed as we do to clear up what we take to be a misunderstanding on others' part, and perhaps equally on ours.[57]

§5. On the Family as Part of the Basic Structure

5.1. To illustrate further the use and scope of public reason, I shall now consider a range of questions about a single institution, the family.[58] I do this by using a particular political conception of justice and

57. I will mention another form of discourse that I call "witnessing": it typically occurs in an ideal, politically well-ordered, and fully just society in which all votes are the result of citizens' voting in accordance with their most reasonable conception of political justice. Nevertheless, it may happen that some citizens feel they must express their principled dissent from existing institutions, policies, or enacted legislation. I assume that Quakers accept constitutional democracy and abide by its legitimate law, yet at the same time may reasonably express the religious basis of their pacifism. (The parallel case of Catholic opposition to abortion is mentioned in §6.1.) Yet witnessing differs from civil disobedience in that it does not appeal to principles and values of a (liberal) political conception of justice. While on the whole these citizens endorse reasonable political conceptions of justice supporting a constitutional democratic society, in this case they nevertheless feel they must not only let other citizens know the deep basis of their strong opposition but must also bear witness to their faith by doing so. At the same time, those bearing witness accept the idea of public reason. While they may think the outcome of a vote on which all reasonable citizens have conscientiously followed public reason to be incorrect or not true, they nevertheless recognize it as legitimate law and accept the obligation not to violate it. In such a society there is strictly speaking no case for civil disobedience and conscientious refusal. The latter requires what I have called a nearly just, but not fully just, society. See *A Theory of Justice,* sec. 55.

58. I have thought that J. S. Mill's landmark *The Subjection of Women* (1869), in *Collected Works of John Stuart Mill,* vol. 21, made clear that a decent liberal conception of justice (including what I called justice as fairness) implied equal justice for women as well as men. Admittedly, *A Theory of Justice* should have been more explicit about this, but that was a fault of mine and not of political liberalism itself. I have been encouraged to think that a liberal account of equal justice for women is viable by Susan

looking at the role that it assigns to the family in the basic structure of society. Since the content of public reason is determined by all the reasonable political conceptions that satisfy the criterion of reciprocity, the range of questions about the family covered by this political conception will indicate the ample space for debate and argument comprehended by public reason as a whole.

The family is part of the basic structure, since one of its main roles is to be the basis of the orderly production and reproduction of society and its culture from one generation to the next. Political society is always regarded as a scheme of social cooperation over time indefinitely; the idea of a future time when its affairs are to be concluded and society disbanded is foreign to the conception of political society. Thus, reproductive labor is socially necessary labor. Accepting this, a central role of the family is to arrange in a reasonable and effective way the raising of and caring for children, ensuring their moral development and education into the wider culture.[59] Citizens must have a sense of justice and the political virtues that support political and social institutions. The family must ensure the nurturing and development of such citizens in appropriate numbers to maintain an enduring society.[60]

These requirements limit all arrangements of the basic structure, including efforts to achieve equality of opportunity. The family imposes

---

Moller Okin, *Justice, Gender, and the Family* (New York: Basic Books, 1989); Linda C. McClain, "'Atomistic Man' Revisited: Liberalism, Connection, and Feminist Jurisprudence," *Southern California Law Review,* 65 (1992): 1171; Martha Nussbaum, *Sex and Social Justice* (Oxford: Oxford University Press, 1998), a collection of her essays from 1990 to 1996, including "The Feminist Critique of Liberalism," her Oxford Amnesty Lecture for 1996; and Sharon A. Lloyd, "Situating a Feminist Criticism of John Rawls's *Political Liberalism,*" *Loyola LA Law Review,* 28 (1995): 1319. I have gained a great deal from their writings.

59. See *A Theory of Justice,* secs. 70–76 (discussing the stages of moral development and their relevance to justice as fairness).

60. However, no particular form of the family (monogamous, heterosexual, or otherwise) is required by a political conception of justice so long as the family is arranged to fulfill these tasks effectively and doesn't run afoul of other political values. Note that this observation sets the way in which justice as fairness deals with the question of gay and lesbian rights and duties, and how they affect the family. If these rights and duties are consistent with orderly family life and the education of children, they are, *ceteris paribus,* fully admissible.

constraints on ways in which this goal can be achieved, and the principles of justice are stated to try to take these constraints into account. I cannot pursue these complexities here, but assume that as children we grow up in a small intimate group in which elders (normally parents) have a certain moral and social authority.

5.2. In order for public reason to apply to the family, it must be seen, in part at least, as a matter for political justice. It may be thought that this is not so, that the principles of justice do not apply to the family and hence those principles do not secure equal justice for women and their children.[61] This is a misconception. It may arise as follows: the primary subject of political justice is the basic structure of society understood as the arrangement of society's main institutions into a unified system of social cooperation over time. The principles of political justice are to apply directly to this structure, but are not to apply directly to the internal life of the many associations within it, the family among them. Thus, some may think that if those principles do not apply directly to the internal life of families, they cannot ensure equal justice for wives along with their husbands.

Much the same question arises in regard to all associations, whether they be churches or universities, professional or scientific associations, business firms or labor unions. The family is not peculiar in this respect. To illustrate: it is clear that liberal principles of political justice do not require ecclesiastical governance to be democratic. Bishops and cardinals need not be elected; nor need the benefits attached to a church's hierarchy of offices satisfy a specified distributive principle, certainly not the difference principle.[62] This shows how the principles of political justice do not apply to the internal life of a church, nor is it desirable, or consistent with liberty of conscience or freedom of association, that they should.

On the other hand, the principles of political justice do impose certain essential constraints that bear on ecclesiastical governance. Churches cannot practice effective intolerance, since, as the principles of justice require, public law does not recognize heresy and apostasy as

---

61. See Okin, *Justice, Gender, and the Family*, pp. 90–93.
62. The difference principle is defined in *A Theory of Justice*, sec. 13.

crimes, and members of churches are always at liberty to leave their faith. Thus, although the principles of justice do not apply directly to the internal life of churches, they do protect the rights and liberties of their members by the constraints to which all churches and associations are subject. This is not to deny that there are appropriate conceptions of justice that do apply directly to most if not all associations and groups, as well as to various kinds of relationships among individuals. Yet these conceptions of justice are not political conceptions. In each case, what is the appropriate conception is a separate and additional question, to be considered anew in each particular instance, given the nature and role of the relevant association, group, or relation.

Now consider the family. Here the idea is the same: political principles do not apply directly to its internal life, but they do impose essential constraints on the family as an institution and so guarantee the basic rights and liberties, and the freedom and opportunities, of all its members. This they do, as I have said, by specifying the basic rights of equal citizens who are the members of families. The family as part of the basic structure cannot violate these freedoms. Since wives are equally citizens with their husbands, they have all the same basic rights, liberties, and opportunities as their husbands; and this, together with the correct application of the other principles of justice, suffices to secure their equality and independence.

To put the case another way, we distinguish between the point of view of people as citizens and their point of view as members of families and of other associations.[63] As citizens we have reasons to impose the constraints specified by the political principles of justice on associations; while as members of associations we have reasons for limiting those constraints so that they leave room for a free and flourishing internal life appropriate to the association in question. Here again we see the need for the division of labor between different kinds of principles. We wouldn't want political principles of justice—including principles of distributive justice—to apply directly to the internal life of the family.

63. I borrow this thought from Joshua Cohen, "Okin on Justice, Gender, and Family," *Canadian Journal of Philosophy,* 22 (1992): 278.

These principles do not inform us how to raise our children, and we are not required to treat our children in accordance with political principles. Here those principles are out of place. Surely parents must follow some conception of justice (or fairness) and due respect with regard to their children, but, within certain limits, this is not for political principles to prescribe. Clearly the prohibition of abuse and neglect of children, and much else, will, as constraints, be a vital part of family law. But at some point society has to rely on the natural affection and goodwill of the mature family members.[64]

Just as the principles of justice require that wives have all the rights of citizens, the principles of justice impose constraints on the family on behalf of children who as society's future citizens have basic rights as such. A long and historic injustice to women is that they have borne, and continue to bear, an unjust share of the task of raising, nurturing, and caring for their children. When they are even further disadvantaged by the laws regulating divorce, this burden makes them highly vulnerable. These injustices bear harshly not only on women but also on their children; and they tend to undermine children's capacity to acquire the political virtues required of future citizens in a viable democratic society. Mill held that the family in his day was a school for male despotism: it inculcated habits of thought and ways of feeling and conduct incompatible with democracy.[65] If so, the principles of justice enjoining a reasonable constitutional democratic society can plainly be invoked to reform the family.

5.3. More generally, when political liberalism distinguishes between political justice that applies to the basic structure and other conceptions of justice that apply to the various associations within that structure, it does not regard the political and the nonpolitical domains as two separate, disconnected spaces, each governed solely by its own distinct principles. Even if the basic structure alone is the primary subject of justice, the principles of justice still put essential restrictions on the family and all other associations. The adult members of families

64. Michael Sandel supposes the two principles of justice as fairness to hold generally for associations, including families. See Michael J. Sandel, *Liberalism and the Limits of Justice* (Cambridge: Cambridge University Press, 1982), pp. 30–34.

65. Mill, *Subjection of Women*, chap. 2, pp. 283–298.

and other associations are equal citizens first: that is their basic position. No institution or association in which they are involved can violate their rights as citizens.

A domain so-called, or a sphere of life, is not, then, something already given apart from political conceptions of justice. A domain is not a kind of space, or place, but rather is simply the result, or upshot, of how the principles of political justice are applied, directly to the basic structure and indirectly to the associations within it. The principles defining the equal basic liberties and opportunities of citizens always hold in and through all so-called domains. The equal rights of women and the basic rights of their children as future citizens are inalienable and protect them wherever they are. Gender distinctions limiting those rights and liberties are excluded.[66] So the spheres of the political and the public, of the nonpublic and the private, fall out from the content and application of the conception of justice and its principles. If the so-called private sphere is alleged to be a space exempt from justice, then there is no such thing.

The basic structure is a single social system, each part of which may influence the rest. Its basic principles of political justice specify all its main parts and its basic rights reach throughout. The family is only one part (though a major part) of the system that produces a social division of labor based on gender over time. Some have argued that discrimination against women in the marketplace is the key to the historical gendered division of labor in the family. The resulting wage differences between the genders make it economically sensible that mothers spend more time with their children than fathers do. On the other hand, some believe that the family itself is the linchpin[67] of gender injustice. However, a liberal conception of justice may have to allow for some traditional gendered division of labor within families—assume, say, that this division is based on religion—provided it is fully voluntary and does not result from or lead to injustice. To say that this division of labor is in this case fully voluntary means that it is adopted by people on the basis of their religion, which from a political point of view is vol-

---

66. See *A Theory of Justice*, sec. 16, p. 99.
67. This is Okin's term. See Okin, *Justice, Gender and the Family*, pp. 6, 14, 170.

untary,[68] and not because various other forms of discrimination elsewhere in the social system make it rational and less costly for husband and wife to follow a gendered division of labor in the family.

Some want a society in which division of labor by gender is reduced to a minimum. But for political liberalism, this cannot mean that such division is forbidden. One cannot propose that equal division of labor in the family be simply mandated, or its absence in some way penalized at law for those who do not adopt it. This is ruled out because the division of labor in question is connected with basic liberties, including the freedom of religion. Thus, to try to minimize gendered division of labor means, in political liberalism, to try to reach a social condition in which the remaining division of labor is voluntary. This allows in principle that considerable gendered division of labor may persist. It is only involuntary division of labor that is to be reduced to zero.

Hence the family is a crucial case for seeing whether the single system—the basic structure—affords equal justice to both men and women. If the gendered division of labor in the family is indeed fully voluntary, then there is reason to think that the single system realizes fair equality of opportunity for both genders.

5.4. Since a democracy aims for full equality for all its citizens, and so of women, it must include arrangements to achieve it. If a basic, if not the main, cause of women's inequality is their greater share in the bearing, nurturing, and caring for children in the traditional division of labor within the family, steps need to be taken either to equalize their share, or to compensate them for it.[69] How best to do this in particular historical conditions is not for political philosophy to decide.

68. On this point, see *Political Liberalism,* lecture VI, sec. 3.2, pp. 221–222. Whether it is properly voluntary, and if so, under what conditions, is a disputed question. Briefly, the question involves the distinction between the reasonable and the rational explained thus: an action is voluntary in one sense, but it may not be voluntary in another. It may be voluntary in the sense of rational: doing the rational thing in the circumstances even when these involve unfair conditions; or an action may be voluntary in the sense of reasonable: doing the rational thing when all the surrounding conditions are also fair. Clearly the text interprets "voluntary" in the second sense: affirming one's religion is voluntary when all of the surrounding conditions are reasonable, or fair. In these remarks I have assumed that the subjective conditions of voluntariness (whatever they may be) are present and have only noted the objective ones. A full discussion would lead us far afield.

69. See Victor R. Fuchs, *Women's Quest for Economic Equality* (Cambridge, Mass.: Harvard University Press, 1988). Chapters 3 and 4 summarize the evidence for saying

But a now common proposal is that as a norm or guideline, the law should count a wife's work in raising children (when she bears that burden as is still common) as entitling her to an equal share in the income that her husband earns during their marriage. Should there be a divorce, she should have an equal share in the increased value of the family's assets during that time.

Any departure from this norm would require a special and clear justification. It seems intolerably unjust that a husband may depart the family taking his earning power with him and leaving his wife and children far less advantaged than before. Forced to fend for themselves, their economic position is often precarious. A society that permits this does not care about women, much less about their equality, or even about their children, who are its future.

The crucial question may be what precisely is covered by gender-structured institutions. How are their lines drawn? If we say the gender system includes whatever social arrangements adversely affect the equal basic liberties and opportunities of women, as well as those of their children as future citizens, then surely that system is subject to critique by the principles of justice. The question then becomes whether the fulfillment of these principles suffices to remedy the gender system's faults. The remedy depends in part on social theory and human psychology, and much else. It cannot be settled by a conception of justice alone.

In concluding these remarks on the family, I should say that I have not tried to argue fully for particular conclusions. Rather, to repeat, I have simply wanted to illustrate how a political conception of justice and its ordering of political values apply to a single institution of the basic structure and can cover many (if not all) of its various aspects. As I have said, these values are given an order within the particular political conception to which they are attached.[70] Among these values are the freedom and equality of women, the equality of children as future citizens, the freedom of religion, and finally, the value of the family in securing the orderly production and reproduction of society and of its

---

the main cause is not, as it is often said, employer discrimination, while chapters 7 and 8 propose what is to be done.

70. See §2.3.

culture from one generation to the next. These values provide public reasons for all citizens. So much is claimed not only for justice as fairness but for any reasonable political conception.

§6. Questions about Public Reason

I now turn to various questions and doubts about the idea of public reason and try to allay them.

6.1. First, it may be objected that the idea of public reason would unreasonably limit the topics and considerations available for political argument and debate, and that we should adopt instead what we may call the open view with no constraints. I now discuss two examples to rebut this objection.

(a) One reason for thinking public reason is too restrictive is to suppose that it mistakenly tries to settle political questions in advance. To explain this objection, let's consider the question of school prayer. It might be thought that a liberal position on this question would deny its admissibility in public schools. But why so? We have to consider all the political values that can be invoked to settle this question and on which side the decisive reasons fall. The famous debate in 1784–1785 between Patrick Henry and James Madison over the establishment of the Anglican Church in Virginia and involving religion in the schools was argued almost entirely by reference to political values alone. Henry's argument for establishment was based on the view that "Christian knowledge hath a natural tendency to correct the morals of men, restrain their vices, and preserve the peace of society, which cannot be effected without a competent provision for learned teachers."[71] Henry did not seem to argue for Christian knowledge as good in itself

71. See Thomas J. Curry, *The First Freedoms: Church and State in America to the Passage of the First Amendment* (Oxford: Oxford University Press, 1986), pp. 139–148. The quoted language, which appears on p. 140, is from the preamble to the proposed "Bill Establishing a Provision for Teachers of the Christian Religion" (1784). Note that the popular Patrick Henry also provided the most serious opposition to Jefferson's "Bill for Establishing Religious Freedom" (1779), which won out when reintroduced in the Virginia Assembly in 1786. Curry, *The First Freedoms*, p. 146.

but rather as an effective way to achieve basic political values, namely, the good and peaceable conduct of citizens. Thus, I take him to mean by "vices," at least in part, those actions contrary to the political virtues found in political liberalism,[72] and expressed by other conceptions of democracy.

Leaving aside the obvious difficulty of whether prayers can be composed that satisfy all the needed restrictions of political justice, Madison's objections to Henry's bill turned largely on whether religious establishment was necessary to support orderly civil society. He concluded it was not. Madison's objections depended also on the historical effects of establishment both on society and on the integrity of religion itself. He was acquainted with the prosperity of colonies that had no establishment, notably Pennsylvania; he cited the strength of early Christianity in opposition to the hostile Roman Empire, and the corruption of past establishments.[73] With some care, many if not all of these arguments can be expressed in terms of the political values of public reason.

Of special interest in the example of school prayer is that it brings out that the idea of public reason is not a view about specific political institutions or policies. Rather, it is a view about the kind of reasons on which citizens are to rest their political cases in making their political justifications to one another when they support laws and policies that invoke the coercive powers of government concerning fundamen-

---

72. For a discussion of these virtues, see *Political Liberalism,* lecture V, sec. 5.4, pp. 194–195.

73. See James Madison, *Memorial and Remonstrance* (1785), in *The Mind of the Founders,* ed. Marvin Meyers (Indianapolis: Bobbs-Merrill, 1973), pp. 8–16. Paragraph 6 refers to the vigor of early Christianity in opposition to the empire, while paragraphs 7 and 11 refer to the mutually corrupting influence of past establishments on both state and religion. In the correspondence between Madison and William Bradford of Pennsylvania, whom he met at Princeton (College of New Jersey), the freedom and prosperity of Pennsylvania without an establishment are praised and celebrated. See *The Papers of James Madison,* vol. 1, ed. William T. Hutchinson and William M. E. Rachal (Chicago: University of Chicago Press, 1962). See especially Madison's letters of 1 December 1773, ibid., pp. 100–101; 24 January 1774, ibid., pp. 104–106; and 1 April 1774, ibid., pp. 111–113. A letter of Bradford's to Madison, 4 March 1774, refers to liberty as the genius of Pennsylvania; ibid., p. 109. Madison's arguments were similar to those of Tocqueville that I mention below. See also Curry, *The First Freedoms,* pp. 142–148.

tal political questions. Also of special interest in this example is that it serves to emphasize that the principles that support the separation of church and state should be such that they can be affirmed by all free and equal citizens, given the fact of reasonable pluralism.

The reasons for the separation of church and state are these, among others: It protects religion from the state and the state from religion; it protects citizens from their churches[74] and citizens from one another. It is a mistake to say that political liberalism is an individualist political conception, since its aim is the protection of the various interests in liberty, both associational and individual. And it is also a grave error to think that the separation of church and state is primarily for the protection of secular culture; of course it does protect that culture, but no more so than it protects all religions. The vitality and wide acceptance of religion in America is often commented upon, as if it were a sign of the peculiar virtue of the American people. Perhaps so, but it may also be connected with the fact that in this country the various religions have been protected by the First Amendment from the state, and none has been able to dominate and suppress the other religions by the capture and use of state power.[75] While some have no doubt

74. It does this by protecting the freedom to change one's faith. Heresy and apostasy are not crimes.

75. What I refer to here is the fact that from the early days of the Emperor Constantine in the fourth century, Christianity punished heresy and tried to stamp out by persecution and religious wars what it regarded as false doctrine (for example, the crusade against the Albigenses led by Innocent III in the thirteenth century). To do this required the coercive powers of the state. Instituted by Pope Gregory IX, the Inquisition was active throughout the Wars of Religion in the sixteenth and seventeenth centuries. While most of the American colonies had known establishments of some kind (Congregationalist in New England, Episcopalian in the South), the United States, thanks to the plurality of its religious sects and the First Amendment which they endorsed, never did. A persecuting zeal has been the great curse of the Christian religion. It was shared by Luther and Calvin and the Protestant Reformers, and it was not radically changed in the Catholic Church until Vatican II. In the Council's Declaration on Religious Freedom—*Dignitatis Humanae*—the Catholic Church committed itself to the principle of religious freedom as found in a constitutional democratic regime. It declared the ethical doctrine of religious freedom resting on the dignity of the human person; a political doctrine with respect to the limits of government in religious matters; and a theological doctrine of the freedom of the Church in its relations to the

entertained that aim since the early days of the Republic, it has not been seriously tried. Indeed, Tocqueville thought that among the main causes of the strength of democracy in this country was the separation of church and state.[76] Political liberalism agrees with many other liberal views in accepting this proposition.[77] Some citizens of faith have felt that this separation is hostile to religion and have sought to change

---

political and social world. All persons, whatever their faith, have the right of religious liberty on the same terms. "Declaration on Religious Freedom *(Dignitatis Humanae):* On the Right of the Person and of Communities to Social and Civil Freedom in Matters Religious" (1965), in Walter Abbott, S.J., ed., *The Documents of Vatican II* (New York: Geoffrey Chapman, 1966), pp. 692–696. As John Courtney Murray, S.J., said: "A longstanding ambiguity had finally been cleared up. The Church does not deal with the secular order in terms of a double standard—freedom for the Church when Catholics are in the minority, privilege for the Church and intolerance for others when Catholics are a majority." John Courtney Murray, "Religious Freedom," in Abbott, ed., *Documents of Vatican II,* p. 673. See also the instructive discussion by Paul E. Sigmund, "Catholicism and Liberal Democracy," in *Catholicism and Liberalism: Contributions to American Public Philosophy,* ed. R. Bruce Douglas and David Hollenbach, S.J. (Cambridge: Cambridge University Press, 1994), especially pp. 233–239.

76. Alexis de Tocqueville, *Democracy in America,* vol. 1, ed. J. P. Mayer, trans. George Lawrence (New York: Perennial Library, 1988), pp. 294–301. In discussing "The Main Causes That Make Religion Powerful in America," Tocqueville says that the Catholic priests "all thought the main reason for the quiet sway of religion over their country was the complete separation of church and state. I have no hesitation in stating that throughout my stay in America I met nobody, lay or cleric, who did not agree about that" (p. 295). He continues: "There have been religions intimately linked to earthly governments, dominating men's souls both by terror and by faith; but when a religion makes such an alliance, I am not afraid to say that it makes the same mistake as any man might; it sacrifices the future for the present, and by gaining a power to which it has no claim, it risks its legitimate authority. . . . Hence religion cannot share the material strength of the rulers without being burdened with some of the animosity roused against them" (p. 297). He remarks that these observations apply all the more to a democratic country, for in that case when religion seeks political power it will attach itself to a particular party and be burdened by hostility to it (p. 298). Referring to the cause of the decline of religion in Europe, he concludes, "I am profoundly convinced that this accidental and particular cause is the close union of politics and religion. . . . European Christianity has allowed itself to be intimately united with the powers of the world" (pp. 300–301). Political liberalism accepts Tocqueville's view and sees it as explaining, so far as possible, the basis of peace among comprehensive doctrines both religious and secular.

77. In this it agrees with Locke, Montesquieu, and Constant; Kant, Hegel, and Mill.

it. In doing this I believe they fail to grasp a main cause of the strength of religion in this country and, as Tocqueville says, seem ready to jeopardize it for temporary gains in political power.

(b) Others may think that public reason is too restrictive because it may lead to a stand-off[78] and fail to bring about decisions on disputed issues. A stand-off in some sense may indeed happen, not only in moral and political reasoning but in all forms of reasoning, including science and common sense. Nevertheless, this is irrelevant. The relevant comparison is to those situations in which legislators enacting laws and judges deciding cases must make decisions. Here some political rule of action must be laid down and all must be able reasonably to endorse the process by which a decision is reached. Recall that public reason sees the office of citizen with its duty of civility as analogous to that of judge with its duty of deciding cases. Just as judges are to decide cases by legal grounds of precedent, recognized canons of statutory interpretation, and other relevant grounds, so citizens are to reason by public reason and to be guided by the criterion of reciprocity, whenever constitutional essentials and matters of basic justice are at stake.

Thus, when there seems to be a stand-off, that is, when legal arguments seem evenly balanced on both sides, judges cannot resolve the case simply by appealing to their own political views. To do that is for judges to violate their duty. The same holds with public reason: if, when stand-offs occur, citizens simply invoke grounding reasons of their comprehensive views,[79] the principle of reciprocity is violated. From the point of view of public reason, citizens must vote for the ordering of political values they sincerely think the most reasonable. Otherwise they fail to exercise political power in ways that satisfy the criterion of reciprocity.

---

78. I take this term from Philip Quinn. The idea appears in *Political Liberalism,* lecture VI, sec. 7.1–2, pp. 240–241.

79. I use the term "grounding reasons" since many who might appeal to these reasons view them as the proper grounds, or the true basis—religious, philosophical, or moral—of the ideals and principles of public reasons and political conceptions of justice.

In particular, when hotly disputed questions, such as that of abortion, arise which may lead to a stand-off between different political conceptions, citizens must vote on the question according to their complete ordering of political values.[80] Indeed, this is a normal case: unanimity of views is not to be expected. Reasonable political conceptions of justice do not always lead to the same conclusion;[81] nor do citizens holding the same conception always agree on particular issues. Yet the outcome of the vote, as I said before, is to be seen as legitimate provided all government officials, supported by other reasonable citizens, of a reasonably just constitutional regime sincerely vote in accordance with the idea of public reason. This doesn't mean the outcome is true or correct, but that it is reasonable and legitimate law, binding on citizens by the majority principle.

Some may, of course, reject a legitimate decision, as Roman Catholics may reject a decision to grant a right to abortion. They may pre-

---

80. Some have quite naturally read the footnote in *Political Liberalism*, lecture VI, sec. 7.2, pp. 243–244, as an argument for the right to abortion in the first trimester. I do not intend it to be one. (It does express my opinion, but my opinion is not an argument.) I was in error in leaving it in doubt whether the aim of the footnote was only to illustrate and confirm the following statement in the text to which the footnote is attached: "The only comprehensive doctrines that run afoul of public reason are those that cannot support a reasonable balance [or ordering] of political values [on the issue]." To try to explain what I meant, I used three political values (of course, there are more) for the troubled issue of the right to abortion to which it might seem improbable that political values could apply at all. I believe a more detailed interpretation of those values may, when properly developed in public reason, yield a reasonable argument. I don't say the most reasonable or decisive argument; I don't know what that would be, or even if it exists. (For an example of such a more detailed interpretation, see Judith Jarvis Thomson, "Abortion," *Boston Review*, 20 [Summer 1995]: 11, though I would want to add several addenda to it.) Suppose now, for purposes of illustration, that there is a reasonable argument in public reason for the right to abortion but there is no equally reasonable balance, or ordering, of the political values in public reason that argues for the denial of that right. Then in this kind of case, but only in this kind of case, does a comprehensive doctrine denying the right to abortion run afoul of public reason. However, if it can satisfy the proviso of the wide public reason better, or at least as well as other views, it has made its case in public reason. Of course, a comprehensive doctrine can be unreasonable on one or several issues without being simply unreasonable.

81. See *Political Liberalism*, lecture VI, sec. 7.1, pp. 240–241.

sent an argument in public reason for denying it and fail to win a majority.[82] But they need not themselves exercise the right to abortion. They can recognize the right as belonging to legitimate law enacted in accordance with legitimate political institutions and public reason, and therefore not resist it with force. Forceful resistance is unreasonable: it would mean attempting to impose by force their own comprehensive doctrine that a majority of other citizens who follow public reason, not unreasonably, do not accept. Certainly Catholics may, in line with public reason, continue to argue against the right to abortion. Reasoning is not closed once and for all in public reason any more than it is closed in any form of reasoning. Moreover, that the Catholic Church's nonpublic reason requires its members to follow its doctrine is perfectly consistent with their also honoring public reason.[83]

I do not discuss the question of abortion in itself since my concern is not with that question but rather to stress that political liberalism does not hold that the ideal of public reason should always lead to a general agreement of views, nor is it a fault that it does not. Citizens learn and profit from debate and argument, and when their arguments

---

82. For such an argument see Cardinal Joseph Bernadin, "The Consistent Ethic: What Sort of Framework?" *Origins,* 16 (October 30, 1986): 347–350. The idea of public order presented by the Cardinal includes these three political values: public peace, essential protections of human rights, and the commonly accepted standards of moral behavior in a community of law. Further, he grants that not all moral imperatives are to be translated into prohibitive civil statutes and thinks it essential to the political and social order to protect human life and basic human rights. The denial of the right to abortion he hopes to justify on the basis of those three values. I don't, of course, assess his argument here, except to say that it is clearly cast in some form of public reason. Whether it is itself reasonable or not, or more reasonable than the arguments on the other side, is another matter. As with any form of reasoning in public reason, the reasoning may be fallacious or mistaken.

83. As far as I can see, this view is similar to Father John Courtney Murray's position about the stand the Church should take in regard to contraception in *We Hold These Truths: Catholic Reflections on the American Proposition* (New York: Sheed and Ward, 1960), pp. 157–158. See also Mario Cuomo's lecture on abortion in his Notre Dame Lecture of 1984, in *More Than Words: The Speeches of Mario Cuomo* (New York: St. Martin's, 1993), pp. 32–51. I am indebted to Leslie Griffin and Paul Weithman for discussion and clarification about points involved in this and the preceding footnote and for acquainting me with Father Murray's view.

follow public reason, they instruct society's political culture and deepen their understanding of one another even when agreement cannot be reached.

6.2. Some of the considerations underlying the stand-off objection lead to a more general objection to public reason, namely, that the content of the family of reasonable political conceptions of justice on which it is based is itself much too narrow. This objection insists that we should always present what we think are true or grounding reasons for our views. That is, the objection insists, we are bound to express the true, or the right, as seen from our comprehensive doctrines.

However, as I said at the beginning, in public reason ideas of truth or right based on comprehensive doctrines are replaced by an idea of the politically reasonable addressed to citizens as citizens. This step is necessary to establish a basis of political reasoning that all can share as free and equal citizens. Since we are seeking public justifications for political and social institutions—for the basic structure of a political and social world—we think of persons as citizens. This assigns to each person the same basic political position. In giving reasons to all citizens we don't view persons as socially situated or otherwise rooted, that is, as being in this or that social class, or in this or that property and income group, or as having this or that comprehensive doctrine. Nor are we appealing to each person's or each group's interests, though at some point we must take these interests into account. Rather, we think of persons as reasonable and rational, as free and equal citizens, with the two moral powers[84] and having, at any given moment, a determinate conception of the good, which may change over time. These features of citizens are implicit in their taking part in a fair system of social cooperation and seeking and presenting public justifications for their judgments on fundamental political questions.

I emphasize that this idea of public reason is fully compatible with the many forms of nonpublic reason.[85] These belong to the internal

---

84. These two powers, the capacity for a conception of justice and the capacity for a conception of the good, are discussed in *Political Liberalism*. See especially lecture I, sec. 3.2, p. 19; lecture II, sec. 7.1, p. 81; lecture III, sec. 3.3, pp. 103–104; lecture III, sec. 4.1, p. 108.

85. Ibid., lecture VI, sec. 4, pp. 223–227.

life of the many associations in civil society, and they are not of course all the same; different nonpublic reasons of different religious associations shared by their members are not those of scientific societies. Since we seek a shareable public basis of justification for all citizens in society, giving justifications to particular persons and groups here and there until all are covered fails to do this. To speak of all persons in society is still too broad, unless we suppose that they are in their nature basically the same. In political philosophy one role of ideas about our nature has been to think of people in a standard, or canonical, fashion so that they might all accept the same kind of reasons.[86] In political liberalism, however, we try to avoid natural or psychological views of this kind, as well as theological or secular doctrines. Accounts of human nature we put aside and rely on a political conception of persons as citizens instead.

6.3. As I have stressed throughout, it is central to political liberalism that free and equal citizens affirm both a comprehensive doctrine and a political conception. However, the relation between a comprehensive doctrine and its accompanying political conception is easily misunderstood.

When political liberalism speaks of a reasonable overlapping consensus of comprehensive doctrines,[87] it means that all of these doctrines, both religious and nonreligious, support a political conception of justice underwriting a constitutional democratic society whose principles, ideals, and standards satisfy the criterion of reciprocity. Thus, all reasonable doctrines affirm such a society with its corresponding political institutions: equal basic rights and liberties for all citizens, including liberty of conscience and the freedom of religion.[88] On the other hand, comprehensive doctrines that cannot support such a dem-

86. Sometimes the term "normalize" is used in this connection. For example, persons have certain fundamental interests of a religious or philosophical kind; or else certain basic needs of a natural kind. Again, they may have a certain typical pattern of self-realization. A Thomist will say that we always desire above all else, even if unknown to ourselves, the *Visio Dei;* a Platonist will say that we strive for a vision of the good; a Marxist will say that we aim for self-realization as species-beings.

87. The idea of such a consensus is discussed at various places in *Political Liberalism.* See especially lecture IV, and consult the index.

88. See ibid., p. xviii (paperback edition).

ocratic society are not reasonable. Their principles and ideals do not satisfy the criterion of reciprocity, and in various ways they fail to establish the equal basic liberties. As examples, consider the many fundamentalist religious doctrines, the doctrine of the divine right of monarchs and the various forms of aristocracy, and, not to be overlooked, the many instances of autocracy and dictatorship.

Moreover, a true judgment in a reasonable comprehensive doctrine never conflicts with a reasonable judgment in its related political conception. A reasonable judgment of the political conception must still be confirmed as true, or right, by the comprehensive doctrine. It is, of course, up to citizens themselves to affirm, revise, or change their comprehensive doctrines. Their doctrines may override or count for naught the political values of a constitutional democratic society. But then the citizens cannot claim that such doctrines are reasonable. Since the criterion of reciprocity is an essential ingredient specifying public reason and its content, political liberalism rejects as unreasonable all such doctrines.

In a reasonable comprehensive doctrine, in particular a religious one, the ranking of values may not be what we might expect. Thus, suppose we call *transcendent* such values as salvation and eternal life— the *Visio Dei*. This value, let's say, is higher, or superior to, the reasonable political values of a constitutional democratic society. These are worldly values and therefore on a different, and as it were lower, plane than those transcendent values. It doesn't follow, however, that these lower yet reasonable values are overridden by the transcendent values of the religious doctrine. In fact, a *reasonable* comprehensive doctrine is one in which they are not overridden; it is the unreasonable doctrines in which reasonable political values are overridden. This is a consequence of the idea of the politically reasonable as set out in political liberalism. Recall that it was said: In endorsing a constitutional democratic regime, a religious doctrine may say that such are the limits God sets to our liberty.[89]

---

89. See §3.2. It is sometimes asked why political liberalism puts such a high value on political values, as if one could only do that by assessing those values in comparison with transcendent values. But this comparison political liberalism does not make, nor does it need to make, as is observed in the text.

A further misunderstanding alleges that an argument in public reason could not side with Lincoln against Douglas in their debates of 1858.[90] But why not? Certainly they were debating fundamental political principles about the rights and wrongs of slavery. Since the rejection of slavery is a clear case of securing the constitutional essential of the equal basic liberties, surely Lincoln's view was reasonable (even if not the most reasonable), while Douglas's was not. Therefore, Lincoln's view is supported by any reasonable comprehensive doctrine. It is no surprise, then, that his view is in line with the religious doctrines of the Abolitionists and the Civil Rights Movement. What could be a better example to illustrate the force of public reason in political life?[91]

6.4. A third general objection is that the idea of public reason is unnecessary and serves no purpose in a well-established constitutional democracy. Its limits and constraints are useful primarily when a society is sharply divided and contains many hostile religious associations and secular groups, each striving to become the controlling political force. In the political societies of the European democracies and the United States these worries, so the objection goes, are idle.

However, this objection is incorrect and sociologically faulty. For without citizens' allegiance to public reason and their honoring the duty of civility, divisions and hostilities between doctrines are bound in time to assert themselves, should they not already exist. Harmony and concord among doctrines and a people's affirming public reason are unhap-

90. On this, see Michael J. Sandel, "Review of *Political Liberalism,*" *Harvard Law Review,* 107 (1994): 1778–1782, and more recently Michael J. Sandel, *Democracy's Discontent: America in Search of a Public Philosophy* (Cambridge, Mass.: Harvard University Press, 1996), pp. 21–23.

91. Perhaps some think that a political conception is not a matter of (moral) right and wrong. If so, that is a mistake and is simply false. Political conceptions of justice are themselves intrinsically moral ideas, as I have stressed from the outset. As such they are a kind of normative value. On the other hand, some may think that the relevant political conceptions are determined by how a people actually establish their existing institutions—the political given, as it were, by politics. Viewed in this light, the prevalence of slavery in 1858 implies that Lincoln's criticisms of it were moral, a matter of right and wrong, and certainly not a matter of politics. To say that the political is determined by a people's politics may be a possible use of the term "political." But then it ceases to be a normative idea, and it is no longer part of public reason. We must hold fast to the idea of the political as a fundamental category and covering political conceptions of justice as intrinsic moral values.

pily not a permanent condition of social life. Rather, harmony and concord depend on the vitality of the public political culture and on citizens' being devoted to and realizing the ideal of public reason. Citizens could easily fall into bitterness and resentment, once they no longer see the point of affirming an ideal of public reason and come to ignore it.

To return to where we began in this section: I do not know how to prove that public reason is not too restrictive, or whether its forms are properly described. I suspect it cannot be done. Yet this is not a serious problem if, as I believe, the large majority of cases fit the framework of public reason, and the cases that do not fit all have special features that both enable us to understand why they should cause difficulty and show us how to cope with them as they arise. This prompts the general questions of whether there are examples of important cases of constitutional essentials and basic justice that do not fit the framework of public reason, and if so, why they cause difficulty. In this essay I do not pursue these questions.

§7. Conclusion

7.1. Throughout, I have been concerned with a torturing question in the contemporary world, namely: Can democracy and comprehensive doctrines, religious or nonreligious, be compatible? And if so, how? At the moment a number of conflicts between religion and democracy raise this question. To answer it political liberalism makes the distinction between a self-standing political conception of justice and a comprehensive doctrine. A religious doctrine resting on the authority of the Church or the Bible is not, of course, a liberal comprehensive doctrine: its leading religious and moral values are not those, say, of Kant or Mill. Nevertheless, it may endorse a constitutional democratic society and recognize its public reason. Here it is basic that public reason is a political idea and belongs to the category of the political. Its content is given by the family of (liberal) political conceptions of justice satisfying the criterion of reciprocity. It does not trespass upon religious beliefs and injunctions insofar as these are consistent with the essential constitutional liberties, including the freedom of religion and liberty of conscience. There is, or need be, no war between religion and democracy. In this respect political liberalism is sharply different from and rejects Enlightenment Liberalism, which historically attacked orthodox Christianity.

The conflicts between democracy and reasonable religious doctrines and among reasonable religious doctrines themselves are greatly mitigated and contained within the bounds of reasonable principles of justice in a constitutional democratic society. This mitigation is due to the idea of toleration, and I have distinguished between two such ideas.[92] One is purely political, being expressed in terms of the rights and duties protecting religious liberty in accordance with a reasonable political conception of justice.[93] The other is not purely political but expressed from within a religious or a nonreligious doctrine. However, a reasonable judgment of the political conception must still be confirmed as true, or right, by a reasonable comprehensive doctrine.[94] I assume, then, that a reasonable comprehensive doctrine accepts some form of the political argument for toleration. Of course, citizens may think that the grounding reasons for toleration and for the other elements of a constitutional democratic society are not political but rather are to be found in their religious or nonreligious doctrines. And these reasons, they may well say, are the true or the right reasons; and they may see the political reasons as superficial, the grounding ones as deep. Yet there is no conflict here, but simply concordant judgments made within political conceptions of justice on the one hand, and within comprehensive doctrines on the other.

92. See §3.2.
93. See *Political Liberalism,* lecture II, secs. 3.2–4, pp. 60–62. The main points can be set out in summary fashion as follows: (1) Reasonable persons do not all affirm the same comprehensive doctrine. This is said to be a consequence of the burdens of judgment. See note 95. (2) Many reasonable doctrines are affirmed, not all of which can be true or right (as judged from within a comprehensive doctrine). (3) It is not unreasonable to affirm any one of the reasonable comprehensive doctrines. (4) Others who affirm reasonable doctrines different from ours are, we grant, reasonable also, and certainly not for that reason unreasonable. (5) In going beyond recognizing the reasonableness of a doctrine and affirming our belief in it, we are not being unreasonable. (6) Reasonable persons think it unreasonable to use political power, should they possess it, to repress other doctrines that are reasonable yet different from their own.
94. See §6.3.

There are limits, however, to reconciliation by public reason. Three main kinds of conflicts set citizens at odds: those deriving from irreconcilable comprehensive doctrines; those deriving from differences in status, class position, or occupation, or from differences in ethnicity, gender, or race; and finally, those deriving from the burdens of judgment.[95] Political liberalism concerns primarily the first kind of conflict. It holds that even though our comprehensive doctrines are irreconcilable and cannot be compromised, nevertheless citizens who affirm reasonable doctrines may share reasons of another kind, namely, public reasons given in terms of political conceptions of justice. I also believe that such a society can resolve the second kind of conflict, which deals with conflicts between citizens' fundamental interests—political, economic, and social. For once we accept reasonable principles of justice and recognize them to be reasonable (even if not the most reasonable), and know, or reasonably believe, that our political and social institutions satisfy them, the second kind of conflict need not arise, or arise so forcefully. Political liberalism does not explicitly consider these conflicts but leaves them to be considered by justice as fairness, or by some other reasonable conception of political justice. Finally, conflicts arising from the burdens of judgment always exist and limit the extent of possible agreement.

7.2. Reasonable comprehensive doctrines do not reject the essentials of a constitutional democratic polity.[96] Moreover, reasonable persons are characterized in two ways: First, they stand ready to offer fair terms of social cooperation between equals, and they abide by these terms if others do also, even should it be to their advantage not to;[97] second, reasonable persons recognize and accept the consequences of the burdens of judgment, which leads to the idea of reasonable toleration in a democratic society.[98] Finally we come to the idea of legitimate law,

---

95. These burdens are discussed in *Political Liberalism,* lecture II, sec. 2. Roughly, they are sources or causes of reasonable disagreement between reasonable and rational persons. They involve balancing the weight of different kinds of evidence and kinds of values, and the like, and they affect both theoretical and practical judgments.

96. Ibid., p. xviii.

97. Ibid., lecture II, sec. 1.1, pp. 49–50.

98. Ibid., lecture II, secs. 2–3.4, pp. 54–62.

which reasonable citizens understand to apply to the general structure of political authority.[99] They know that in political life unanimity can rarely if ever be expected, so a reasonable democratic constitution must include majority or other plurality voting procedures in order to reach decisions.[100]

The idea of the politically reasonable is sufficient unto itself for the purposes of public reason when basic political questions are at stake. Of course, fundamentalist religious doctrines and autocratic and dictatorial rulers will reject the ideas of public reason and deliberative democracy. They will say that democracy leads to a culture contrary to their religion, or denies the values that only autocratic or dictatorial rule can secure.[101] They assert that the religiously true, or the philosophically true, overrides the politically reasonable. We simply say that such a doctrine is politically unreasonable. Within political liberalism nothing more need be said.

I noted in the beginning[102] the fact that every actual society, however dominant and controlling its reasonable citizens may be, will normally contain numerous unreasonable doctrines that are not compatible with a democratic society—either certain religious doctrines, such as fundamentalist religions, or certain nonreligious (secular) doctrines, such as those of autocracy and dictatorship, of which our century offers hideous examples. How far unreasonable doctrines may be active and are to be tolerated in a constitutional democratic regime does not present a new and different question, despite the fact that in this account of public reason we have focused on the idea of the reasonable and the role of reasonable citizens. There is not one account of toleration for reasonable doctrines and another for unreasonable ones. Both cases are settled by the appropriate political principles of justice and the conduct those principles permit.[103] Unreasonable doctrines

---

99. Ibid., lecture IV, secs. 1.2–3, pp. 135–137.

100. Ibid., lecture IX, sec. 2.1, p. 393.

101. Observe that neither the religious objection to democracy nor the autocratic one could be made by public reasoning.

102. See note 3.

103. See *A Theory of Justice*, sec. 35 (on toleration of the intolerant); *Political Liberalism*, lecture V, sec. 6.2, pp. 197–199.

are a threat to democratic institutions, since it is impossible for them to abide by a constitutional regime except as a *modus vivendi.* Their existence sets a limit to the aim of fully realizing a reasonable democratic society with its ideal of public reason and the idea of legitimate law. This fact is not a defect or failure of the idea of public reason, but rather it indicates that there are limits to what public reason can accomplish. It does not diminish the great value and importance of attempting to realize that ideal to the fullest extent possible.

7.3. I end by pointing out the fundamental difference between *A Theory of Justice* and *Political Liberalism.* The first explicitly attempts to develop from the idea of the social contract, represented by Locke, Rousseau, and Kant, a theory of justice that is no longer open to objections often thought fatal to it, and that proves superior to the long dominant tradition of utilitarianism. *A Theory of Justice* hopes to present the structural features of such a theory so as to make it the best approximation to our considered judgments of justice and hence to give the most appropriate moral basis for a democratic society. Furthermore, justice as fairness is presented there as a comprehensive liberal doctrine (although the term "comprehensive doctrine" is not used in the book) in which all the members of its well-ordered society affirm that same doctrine. This kind of well-ordered society contradicts the fact of reasonable pluralism and hence *Political Liberalism* regards that society as impossible.

Thus, *Political Liberalism* considers a different question, namely: How is it possible for those affirming a comprehensive doctrine, religious or nonreligious, and in particular doctrines based on religious authority, such as the Church or the Bible, also to hold a reasonable political conception of justice that supports a constitutional democratic society? The political conceptions are seen as both liberal and self-standing and not as comprehensive, whereas the religious doctrines may be comprehensive but not liberal. The two books are asymmetrical, though both have an idea of public reason. In the first, public reason is given by a comprehensive liberal doctrine, while in the second, public reason is a way of reasoning about political values shared by free and equal citizens that does not trespass on citizens' comprehensive doctrines so long as those doctrines are consistent with a democratic polity. Thus, the well-ordered constitutional democratic society of *Political Liberalism* is one in which the dominant and controlling citizens affirm and act from irreconcilable yet reasonable comprehensive doctrines. These doctrines in turn support reasonable political conceptions—although not necessarily the most reasonable—which specify the basic rights, liberties, and opportunities of citizens in society's basic structure.

Index